Lancashire Cricket at the Top

The authors, Vernon Addison, *top*, and Brian Bearshaw.

# Lancashire Cricket at the Top

*Vernon Addison and Brian Bearshaw*

STANLEY PAUL
*London*

STANLEY PAUL & CO LTD
*178–202 Great Portland Street, London W1*

AN IMPRINT OF THE HUTCHINSON GROUP

London Melbourne Sydney
Auckland Johannesburg Cape Town
and agencies throughout the world

*First published* 1971

*Acknowledgments*

The authors wish to acknowledge the use of photographs from the following: Manchester Evening News; Daily Express; Sport and General; Hallawell Photos, Manchester; R. Butterworth, Ashton-under-Lyne; Press Association and Jack Hickes, Leeds. For statistical background they are also indebted to assistance from Manchester neswpaper librarian H. Montgomery.

*This book has been set in Imprint type, printed in Great Britain by offset litho at Taylor Garnett Evans & Co Ltd, Watford, Herts bound by William Brendon, at Tiptree, Essex*

ISBN 0 09 1075505

# Contents

# Foreword
## by Jack Bond

As LANCASHIRE enter the 1971 season I cannot help thinking of a schoolmaster in the obscurity of the backwoods of Norfolk.

While I have the good fortune to be captain of Lancashire— John Player League champions of 1969 and '70, and Gillette Cup holders—I could so easily have been that master.

Wes Hall, the West Indies fast bowler did more than break my left arm when one of his express deliveries smashed into me in 1963; he put a question mark against my cricketing future. It's not that I lost confidence in myself but rather that I felt that others lost confidence in me at Old Trafford.

So in the close season of 1964–65 I came very near to leaving Lancashire. I had been interviewed for a position as sportsmaster to a boys school in the Eastern Counties and the job was mine.

Fortunately I hesitated. I thought of my benefit which would soon be due. Money has never been my primary concern but, after all, I had earned the benefit and you don't often get the chance of being rewarded for services rendered with a substantial lump sum. A three-year winter coaching stint in South Africa with a school in Kimberley also helped to give me a new lease of life. I turned out with the boys when they played men's teams in senior league matches and it helped refresh my enthusiasm.

So I stayed with Lancashire and how glad I am for now we are hoping to bring success to the county for the third year on the run. People keep saying to me as the new season grows near. 'What's it like starting off with three titles behind you in two years?'

The answer is: no different to how I would feel as captain of any of the other 16 counties. It was great winning those trophies but that is past. We all start on the same footing and you are only as good as your last match.

What are we aiming for this season? Well, of course, we will try for the lot. It would be great to go down in the record books as Player League champions for the first three years it was held; a Gillette Cup double is something to be revered; but the big one is undoubtedly the county championship. Nor do we want to win it just for itself but in a way that will appeal to the public.

'Ah, yes,' I am often told, 'you have the batsmen but what about the bowlers?' Well, I have a theory about the championship. Think of some of the great teams of recent years, Yorkshire before the war, Surrey soon after the war, Worcester when they won the title twice on the run, Kent last year and Glamorgan the season before. They all had one thing in common—a left-hand bowler, generally a spinner. The names? Hedley Verity, Tony Lock, Norman Gifford, Derek Underwood and Malcolm Nash.

Lancashire's big decline started after Malcolm Hilton retired in 1961, after which we didn't have a left hand spinner until David Hughes came along. Overnight successes are rare in the world of spin bowling and David has been three years learning his trade in the first team. At first he had the advantage of being second spinner to the experienced John Savage, but last year he had the number one position thrust upon him and he responded well. This season he has the chance of really blossoming out.

What many people don't realise is that we haven't seen the best of our bowlers yet. For instance Peter Lever and Ken Shuttleworth must be better this summer for having been on the winter tour of Australia. So, too will Jimmy Cumbes with all the first-class experience he was able to get at Surrey after having had few opportunities at Old Trafford. His return is welcome as it adds depth to our bowling. Jack Simmons has tended to be overshadowed but he has picked up vital wickets, such as clean-bowling Colin Cowdrey last season. Then, fortunate captain that I am, I have the choice of no fewer than three more bowlers. Barry Wood's bowling developed so much last season that he has claims to be being called an all-rounder, while Clive Lloyd and Johnny Sullivan are more than useful stand-breakers. As if that's not enough our fielding is worth another bowler.

The present system of bonus points helps our bid for the championship for no side is better equipped to plunder the batting points than we are with Barry Wood, David Lloyd and Harry Pilling to be relied on for the good start on which Clive Lloyd.

Farokh Engineer, Frank Hayes, Johnny Sullivan and Co. can build. The poor old skipper hardly gets a look in.

I have dealt only, you will have realised, with the present and future. That's why I am delighted to have the privilege of introducing this book for it is primarily about the Lancashire of today.

There is too much looking back in cricket. However great were the stars of yesteryear they are not going to help Lancashire's bid for further success this year, nor can they help in the continued return of the crowds to Old Trafford.

Don't tell me either that there are no characters in the game today. Brian Bearshaw and Vernon Addison successfully disprove this theory with rich anecdotes in their commentary on our side of the seventies.

*Chapter 1*

# From Hornby to Bond
*by Brian Bearshaw*

FOUR faceless office blocks watch over the Old Trafford practice ground, impersonal yet commanding, like eunuchs at the entrance of a harem.

Faceless, but not nameless, for they are reminders of the glories that have been Lancashire. The immediate past is recalled in Statham House. Washbrook and Duckworth Houses connect us with the period between the wars, while the House of MacLaren—I dearly wish I could have seen this majestic, stylish player—can take us back to the nineteenth century.

Just across the road from Old Trafford are two short streets standing alongside one another which can easily be overlooked by the supporters who hurry to and from the ground by way of Warwick Road. But unlike the four concrete columns a few hundred yards away, they are blessed with character. Trees stand in front of the terraced houses in Hornby Road and Barlow Road, reminders of the days in Lancashire's history that are now almost beyond human recall.

Hornby and Barlow, given everlasting life in a poem, a beautiful poem by Francis Thompson that captures all the sadness he felt in being away from his much loved county. It is called 'At Lord's':

It is little I repair to the matches of the Southron folk,
Though my own red roses there may blow;
It is little I repair to the matches of the Southron folk,
Though the red roses crest the caps I know.
For the field is full of shades as I near the shadowy coast,

*Top:* Len Hopwood, the last Lancashire player to do the double of 100 wickets and 1,000 runs, looks at the ball with which he took nine Leicester wickets for 33 runs in 1933.
*Above:* Ringing in a new season at Old Trafford is Harry Makepeace who was starting his 46th year with Lancashire when this picture was taken in 1951.

And a ghostly batsman plays to the bowling of a ghost,
And I look through my tears on a soundless-clapping host
As the run-stealers flicker to and fro,
To and fro—
O my Hornby and my Barlow long ago!

Lancashire was formed in 1864, an extension of the Manchester Club that had been in existence for many, many years, and which had already been playing for seven years at the present Old Trafford cricket ground.

Hornby first played for Lancashire in 1867 and became the more famous of the illustrious pair. He started his county career four years before Barlow and played eight more years after his partner retired in 1891. And he was captain of Lancashire in 16 seasons, a record unsurpassed by any of his 17 successors.

But for me, Richard Gorton Barlow's character is much the stronger. It could be that his ghost occasionally walks the same road as me, for he is buried not a mile from my home in Blackpool. His body was laid to rest at Layton Cemetery with an unusual, faintly comical headstone that strikes you as pompous when you discover that Barlow himself designed it and paid for it long before he died in 1919.

Barlow lies close to the main gate under an overpowering stone that shows a set of stumps with the ball passing through middle and leg—a right good ball it looks, too—one bail falling, and three heart-rending words . . . 'Bowled at Last.' Not a bad memorial to a man who carried his bat through the innings 50 times.

A vain man, he made sure the words did him justice. 'Here lie the remains of Richard Gorton Barlow, died 31 July 1919, aged 68 years. For 21 seasons a playing member of the Lancashire County XI and for 21 seasons an umpire in county matches. He also made three journeys to Australia with English teams. This is a consecutive record in first-class cricket which no other cricketer has yet achieved.' Barlow would have liked to have added much more, but alas there wasn't room.

What a character! A man whose iron, North Country spirit, whose uncompromising attitude showed in his cricket, a thoroughly professional player, another hardened Northerner who didn't believe in walking and had no compunction in running out a batsman backing up too far.

He scored only two centuries for his county—both in 1885— but his defensive qualities as an opening batsman were outstanding.

They were infuriating, too, especially on the day in 1882 at Nottingham when he carried his bat through the innings for five not out in 2½ hours. The term stonewaller originated here when the Notts bowler, Barnes, said to Barlow after his innings: 'Bowling at thee were like bowling at a stone wall.'

My own favourite story concerning Barlow was told in the book he wrote in 1908 on 'Forty Seasons of First-Class Cricket'. In a match in which he played at Burley, Yorkshire, one of the umpires was a man with a wooden leg. While this umpire was standing at square leg, the batsman hit the ball with great force in his direction. The unfortunate umpire was unable to get out of the way and the ball struck his wooden leg, snapping it in half like a carrot. The man wavered a moment and then slowly, almost gracefully, toppled over. Some of the players had to pick him up and carry him to the pavilion, from where he was sent home in a cab.

A son of Barlow still lives in Southport, where he has collected many of his father's treasures, including a beautifully-designed silver cup presented to Barlow by W. G. Grace, and three highly-treasured bats, one of which went round the world with Barlow and with which he scored over 4,000 runs.

Barlow also had a daughter whose son, Leslie Barlow Wilson—the initials were contrived purposely by the cricket-loving family—lives in Blackpool, and recalls the walls of his grandfather's home being so full of photographs and momentoes you could not get a pin between them.

Hornby and Barlow were the opening pair in 1881 when Lancashire won the championship for the first time. They were fine openers, stealing runs consistently and cheekily. As Francis Thompson said: 'Run-stealers flickering to and fro.' But Barlow used to say of his captain: 'He tires you out, then he runs you out, then he gives you a guinea.'

Lancashire cricket in those years to the turn of the century must have been a sight to behold. Certainly there was plenty of enthusiasm and such encouragement as a crowd which topped 17,000 one Saturday in 1878 when Gloucestershire and her Graces—W. G., E. M., and G. F.—played at Old Trafford. Lorries were brought on to the ground to serve as stands. People arrived in carriages, on horseback, on foot, or by train, alighting at Old Trafford Station and using the path through the fields.

Wonderful days indeed with Hornby captaining Lancashire in both their nineteenth century championship successes—in 1881 and 1897—and in two of the three years they were joint champions. In

*Top left:* Howzat . . . and that's another victim to George Duckworth.
*Top right:* Enjoying a joke is Eddie Paynter.
*Above:* Here's a line-up to test your memory. Recognise them? Left to right they are Frank Sibbles, Len Hopwood, Dick Tyldesley, Jack Iddon and Charlie Hallows.

*Top left:* One of the famous Tyldesley's, Ernest.
*Above:* Celebration time for Lancashire in 1928 at a party thrown by Johnny Walker's. Left to right round the table are: Len Hopwood, Malcolm Taylor (standing), Frank Sibbles, a Walker's representative, Leonard Green, a rep, Dick Tyldesley, another rep, Charlie Hallows, Ernie Moore (scorer), rep, Harry Makepeace, rep, George Duckworth and Max Halliday.
*Top right:* The legendary Archie MacLaren demonstrates his footwork as he jumps out to drive.

1895 Lancashire scored her highest innings total, an incredible 801 of which MacLaren scored 424 in just under eight hours. What a week that must have been for Somerset, for in the previous match Essex had scored 693.

Manchester-born MacLaren stands high among the great Lancashire players. Any team picked from the 500 men who have represented the county in its 107 years would have to include this batsman of class and grace, this man whose very stance was a pleasure to see. He played 35 times for England, figures surpassed by only two other Lancastrians, Brian Statham and Cyril Washbrook. 'He was a glorious batsman to watch,' Rex Pogson wrote of him. 'With his upright stance, full square to the bowler, and his high lift of the bat and full follow through.'

MacLaren captained Lancashire in her next outright championship win in 1904 and continued to play for the county until the outbreak of the First World War in 1914, when he was 43 years old. But the playing career of Archibald Charles MacLaren—there's a fine Scots sounding name if you like—was not over. In his last innings in first-class cricket he scored 200 not out in $4\frac{1}{2}$ hours for the MCC against New Zealand in Wellington . . . at the age of 51. What a way to go!

Later MacLaren coached the aspiring young men of Lancashire. 'A great coach' was the verdict of Len Hopwood, the last Lancastrian to achieve the double of 1,000 runs and 100 wickets in a season, and who served under MacLaren at Old Trafford. 'He didn't coach cricket into one', he wrote last year in a series of articles on his career. 'By some mysterious means he drew talent out, then developed it. Sometimes he coaxed, at other times he bullied.'
Hopwood told of an occasion at the nets when MacLaren stood in the umpire's position and commanded Hopwood to spin the ball. 'I suppose I had at that time what used to be called the left-hander's natural spin. That indeed was all I knew about spin. I bowled and bowled. More insistent became the demands to "spin it". Finally, and in a thunderous tone, he roared: "Spin the bloody ball." It was the first time I had heard him swear. I was galvanised into action. The next ball turned. I had spun it. So did the next and the next. MacLaren walked away, satisfied.

'Here was an example of MacLaren's technique. He did not try to teach one to spin the ball as others spun it. He made one think for oneself and arrive at an individual solution by trial and error.

'The news that he was to leave Old Trafford was a shock to the young players. But it was inevitable I suppose. MacLaren was by nature intended to be master, never servant. There must have been innumerable clashes of will between committee and coach. Never will I forget his final words on the subject. "The Lancashire committee mustn't think they own me body and soul because they pay me a paltry £550 a year," he was heard to declare.' And that was nearly 50 years ago.

Despite being blessed with such players of the calibre of Brearley, Dean, MacLaren, Sharp, Spooner and Johnnie Tyldesley, Lancashire had to wait 22 years before they could repeat the title success of 1904. It had been a long time, but in the 1920s a team developed that is undoubtedly the best Lancashire have known, and one that stands comparison with any team any county can produce this century. This team won the title four times in five years—1926, 1927, 1928 and 1930—and was second in 1929.

Eight players formed the backbone of all four winning teams. Five were capped by England—Charles Hallows, Ernest Tyldesley, Jack Iddon, Richard Tyldesley and George Duckworth—one by Australia, Ted McDonald, and only Frank Sibbles and Frank Watson failed to reach this distinction. In any other era, less rich in county cricketers, they would unquestionably have played for England.

In those four seasons, McDonald, furiously fast and who had wrecked England with the touring Australians in 1921, took 623 wickets. Yes, that's right . . . 623 in four seasons. Dick Tyldesley, a round, happy gentleman, claimed 472 as Lancashire pushed the opposition to one side as they hastened to the title. Incidentally in 1929, McDonald took 142 wickets for Lancashire and Tyldesley 154.

In three of the seasons Harry Makepeace, another Test player, helped to provide the rocklike foundation of the batting, a formidable little man who believed, like Barlow 50 years before him, that defence was of prime importance in a batsman's make-up.

Major Leonard Green also played in three of the elevens, the first three, his ONLY three years as captain, which must be some sort of a record. Peter Eckersley was in command for the 1930 achievement.

Such a great team and in Ernest Tyldesley they had the man who has scored more runs for Lancashire than anybody else—34,222 for a consistently high average of over 45.

Of the four years 1928 was probably the most outstanding. For Lancashire did not lose a match. It was a remarkable year, too, for Hallows, a prolific, reliable, left-handed batsman who in this season scored 1,000 runs in May. And as any stickler for facts will tell you, that while six batsmen have made 1,000 runs before June, only three

A blazer in the fashion of the day. A. N. Hornby felt the height of
elegance in it, even if he did have to turn back a cuff.

*Top:* Peter Eckersley leads Lancashire out against Kent on May 18th 1932.
*Above:* County Champions 1930 (*standing*) G. Duckworth, F. Watson,
J. L. Hopwood, J. Iddon, F. Sibbles, G. M. Taylor, E. Paynter, (*sitting*)
C. Hallows, E. A. Mc Dnoald, P. T. Eckersley, E. Tyldesley, R. Tyldesley.

actually scored 1,000 in the month of May. And those were W. G. Grace, Walter Hammond, and Hallows. Tom Hayward started on 16 April, Don Bradman who achieved it twice, started on 30 April on both occasions, while Bill Edrich, whose runs were all scored at Lord's in 1938, also started on the last day in April.

Hallows, 76 this year, still lives in Bolton, close to Lancashire's present captain, Jack Bond. His 1,000 runs were scored in 11 innings in 27 days and were completed on the last day of the month. He scored 100, 101, 51 not out, 123, 101 not out, 22, 74, 104, 58, and 34 not out, and when the match against Sussex started on May 30, he was still 232 runs away. Who would have dreamed he could have reached this target? He batted the whole of the first day for 190 not out, and left the ground knowing that only 42 more were needed on the Thursday morning.

Hallows slept badly that Wednesday night, and wasted no time getting to the ground the following morning, as if he needed reassurance from the scoreboard that it wasn't all a dream. He got the 42 he needed, went giddy with the realisation, and was out next ball, caught Jim Parks, bowled Arthur Gilligan.

Lancashire again took the title in 1934, and again under Eckersley, but in the 36 years since then have been top of the championship table only once—and then they had to share it with Surrey in 1950.

There was no shortage of good players after the war, and two of their most illustrious names, Washbrook and Statham, played together for some time. In the last 25 years such outstanding cricketers as Bob Barber, Tommy Greenhough, Bob Berry, Ken Grieves, Ken Higgs, Johnny Ikin, Roy Tattersall, Malcolm Hilton, Geoff Pullar, Winston Place, Alan Wharton, Dick Pollard, Geoff Edrich, Peter Marner, David Green, Eddie Phillipson, have toiled to make Lancashire outright champions once again. Last year Lancashire finished third. Maybe the championship is just around the corner . . .

*Chapter 2*

# Rhoades, the reluctant rebel
## *by Vernon Addison*

THE chief hobby of Cedric Rhoades, chairman of Lancashire, is Roman history. But at cricket he looks back no further than the last match and he far prefers talking about the future.

Within the last year he re-read Gibbons' *Decline and Fall of the Roman Empire*. It took rather longer, however, to arrest the decline of Lancashire's cricketing fortunes.

The first shot that Rhoades fired over the bows of the old order at Old Trafford was at the end of the annual general meeting of 1963 . . . and it hardly made a ripple. Annoyed at the off-hand way questioners were dealt with, he warned the committee: 'If I have my way we will call a special meeting and have you all thrown out.'

Rhoades' outburst made such little impact that a year later some friends confessed they couldn't remember him saying it and even the newspapers, always searching for an angle to enliven what they knew to be a dull event, didn't think this short outburst worth bothering about. Well, they laughed at Disraeli when he first spoke in the House of Commons but they soon had to take notice of him.

So it was with the then unknown Rhoades. He had only been a Lancashire and Cheshire League cricketer with Levenshulme, where he was an opening bat, (highest score 78) and a wicket-keeper (once took seven catches in a match and another time six catches) but he was doing his homework thoroughly in his study of Lancashire cricket, for he and his father rarely missed a match within 100-miles of Lancashire. 'I saw more cricket than half the committee,' he said.

All the time Rhoades was becoming more infuriated with the way the club was being run. The side had great players but was never a

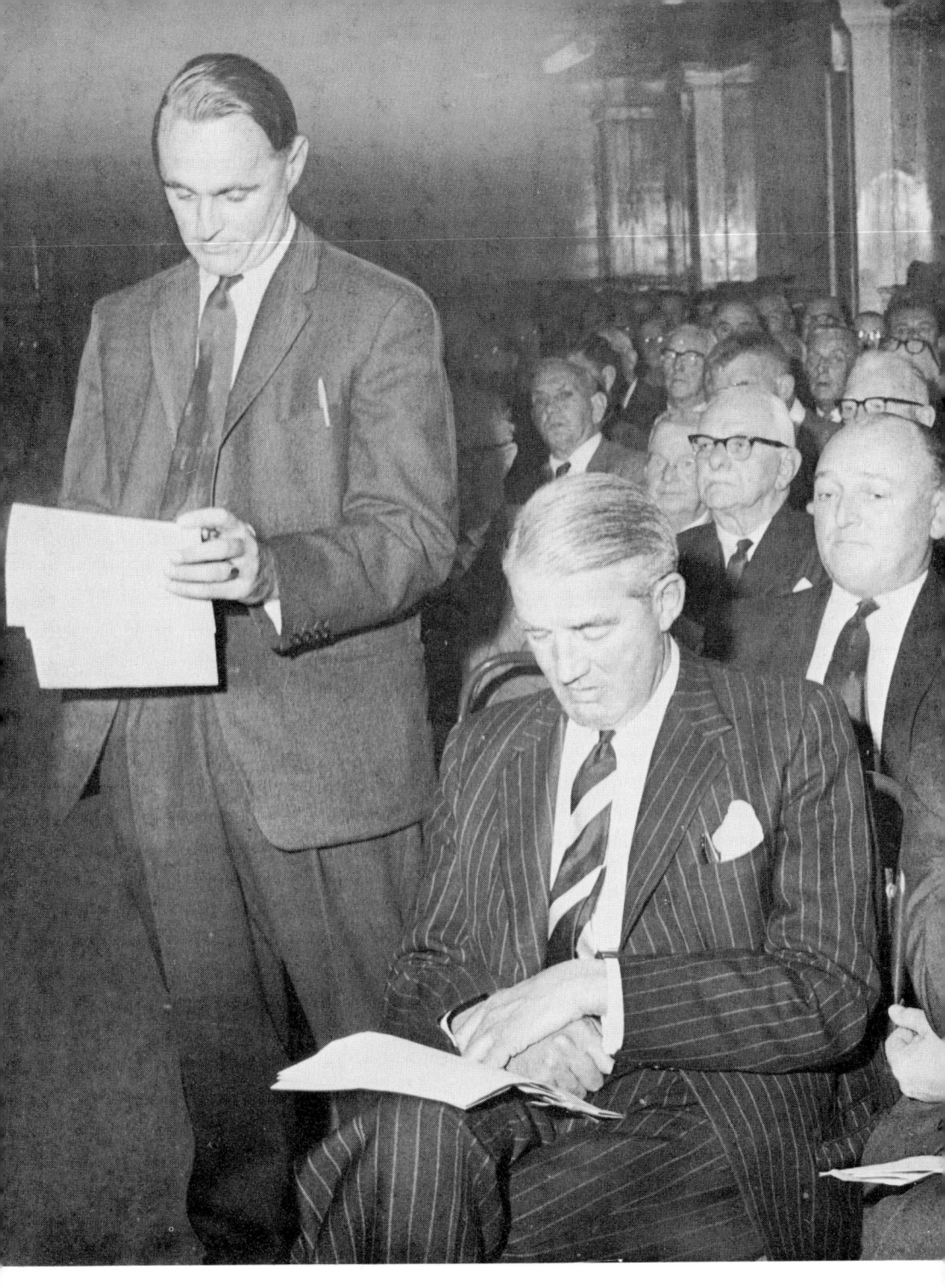

Cedric Rhoades addressing the famous meeting in Houldsworth Hall
which led to the resignation of the Lancashire committee.

team while the committee were aloof.

'You never saw them mixing with ordinary members and when you questioned them you couldn't get satisfactory answers. They had no idea of public relations, press relations or team relations.'

The last straw came in May 1964, when Lancashire were humiliated by Yorkshire at Headingley, being bowled out for 57 to lose by 10 wickets. 'Something had to be done,' said Rhoades.

Soon afterwards John Kay, the indefatigable *Manchester Evening News* cricket writer, added to his long list of major scoops when he revealed that Rhoades was demanding a special meeting for which he needed 50 signatures. Cedric made only one mistake—he forgot to tell his wife. 'As soon as the afternoon editions were out the phone at home hardly stopped ringing with people offering to sign. My wife knew nothing about it and wondered what on earth was going on.'

There was no difficulty in getting the required signatures and by the end of August feeling was running very high with yet another Kay revelation that skipper Ken Grieves, Peter Marner, Geoff Clayton and Jack Dyson were to be sacked. Lancashire officials remained smug in their belief that they knew how to handle trouble-makers. Nevertheless they foresaw that they were unlikely to come out whiter than white from a public washday of dirty linen and suggested that a leading group of the critics should meet them privately. Rhoades put it to his backers, but to a man they replied: 'The public meeting must go on.'

So, on 24 September 1964, Manchester's Houldsworth Hall was, according to Eric Todd in *The Guardian* 'so filled that there appeared to be far more members than were usually to be seen at a county match at Old Trafford'.

It could be added that they were to see a higher calibre performance than they were used to at the cricket ground in those days for Rhoades gave a virtuoso display of shrewdness and oratory.

He wasn't a rebel, he opened, for he stressed that he was merely acting within the framework of the articles of the club's constitution. Unlike rebels he did not offer instant success on the playing field nor fall into the mistake of ranting like a demented preacher.

In a calm voice he catalogued his criticisms ranging from the dismissals of Grieves, Clayton, Dyson and Marner to leakages of information, from the captaincies of Joe Blackledge and Bob Barber to the lack of team spirit. When, raising his tone a little, he demanded: 'If the committee cannot discipline itself how can they discipline the team?' he was halted by a burst of applause.

'Instead of spending so much money on the wonderful ground

at Old Trafford the club—surely it is not a property development company?—could with advantage pay higher wages or give longer contracts.'

Perhaps this last paragraph wasn't the type to bring the audience to their feet but it is significant for it shows the depth of Rhoades' foresight, this becoming the cornerstone of the policy which has since built up the team spirit—so clearly a major factor in the successes of the last two years. It's a policy which many counties still fail to appreciate even over at Yorkshire where they believe they know everything there is to know about cricket, but where they still hire their players on a yearly basis.

Rhoades spoke for only about 15 minutes—again short commons for revolutionaries—but he had put his case so well that even president Canon F. Paton-Williams congratulated him. Tommy Burrows, the club chairman, had to confess that he had never known team spirit to be so low, with members of the second team asking not to be selected for the first eleven.

Another compliment on Rhoades' display came when Dick Bowman, something of a pillar of society as a former Oxford Blue and Lancashire bowler and now successful businessman, said: 'I expected some mud-slinging, but I didn't expect it to come from the committee.'

So it was no surprise that the historic resolution: 'That this meeting is dissatisfied with the conduct of the cricketing affairs of the club' was passed by the overwhelming margin of 656 to 48.

The message of that voting was clear enough: *no* confidence. Yet there was much dithering before the committee resigned en bloc and before the new elections they were to enact one more piece of crass folly, advertising for a captain. There, incredibly, in the middle of *The Times* agony column, it read:

'A first class county cricket club invites applications from persons with first class cricket experience for the position of captain of the county XI. The position will carry a salary in accordance with experience and an allowance to cover expenses.'

A box number was given but once again it was John Kay who revealed that the county was Lancashire—and yet another storm broke. Ken Grieves described it as 'an insult to Brian Statham'; the *Daily Express* quoted a member as saying: 'It's almost too fantastic to believe', while Rhoades warned: 'It's high-handed as the club is in the hands of the members until the annual general meeting in three weeks. It is sheer cheek.'

By then Rhoades was one of 29 members standing for the 12

committee seats although he has always insisted that his only aim was to get things moving. His supporters, however, told him: 'If you make a song and dance then it's up to you to try and do something to put things right.'

He was duly elected and had immediate success, removing vice-presidents from committees and cutting out co-options except in extreme cases, two factors which had made a mockery of the club's elections. Further progress was hard and Rhoades, in his own words, came 'very, very, very close to resigning', but was talked out of it by a few close friends.

Eventually his determination and patience paid off and his ideas began to become accepted. 'I think the change came,' he said, 'when they found out that I wasn't a rocket who would fizzle out and that I wasn't out for myself but only to improve Lancashire cricket. Anyway they were beginning to see that my ideas would work'.

'It was a hell of a fight, though,' he added, but the reluctant rebel became so much accepted that in 1967 he became vice-chairman and in 1969 chairman. In that year the team became the first winners of the John Player Sunday League, while the following year they retained it, adding the Gillette Cup for good measure, the first time the club had lifted the knock-out trophy.

'The results have been most pleasing,' said Rhoades, but firmly added. 'We can't be satisfied with two years success. I will only feel that we have got anywhere when we have been at the top for 10 years.'

In particular he wants to ensure that sport's greatest failing doesn't happen at Lancashire—a successful team growing old together, leaving gaps before the next generation come through.

So he spends as much time as possible encouraging schools cricket. One of his less publicised innovations four years ago was to split the county into eight sections. Whenever the team is playing on a Saturday boys from one of these areas go on an organised visit to Old Trafford. It is rather like looking round a stately home, for they are shown through all sections of the club, and end up watching the players practise at the nets and then the game itself. In the first year about 700 boys came and by last year the figure had risen to 1,600.

Unlike stately homes, however, there are no 'Keep off the grass' signs and more boys are now playing there than ever before.

To Rhoades one of the finest—and most heartening—sights last season was staging an under-13 competition on the main ground, some of the players being so young that they wore shorts. He believes it so important to encourage the players—and spectators—of the future that he tries to see every schoolboy match at the ground.

Unfortunately cricket has become a casualty of the pressures of modern education and in some North-West schools it has been dropped altogether and in many others it doesn't get the same attention as soccer does in the winter. That's a situation that the chairman won't accept, so be warned you PE and teacher-training colleges, he plans to find out why you don't plug cricket more!

His ambition is to turn Old Trafford into a Real Madrid of cricket, open all the year round and staging every kind of sport with the accent on youth. Unlike so many of his age he won't criticise today's youngsters but looks for the reason and a remedy for their troubles. 'They haven't sufficient to occupy them and we must make our club their focal point.'

Finance is an obvious problem and he believes the government should help. 'Compared to some countries on the Continent we are lagging terribly over sports centres and I believe that any Minister for Sport would be short-sighted not to help with money.'

On the question of finance he wants to see Lancashire independent of gates raising enough money from other sources to drive away the worries of the county's notorious weather so that turnstile receipts become a welcome bonus. 'We are 60 per cent of the way there,' he added.

Rhoades is different from so many sporting club chairmen because he does not try to take any credit for the team's success this past two years. Yet he surely laid the foundation with such shrewd eye to detail, like giving the skipper the right to take out the team that he wants; the security of the longer contracts and erasing the dread of playing for your place by telling promoted players that they are in for three matches whatever happens in the first one.

Rhoades is so refreshing that he could have blown fresh air through the beard of W. G. Grace, whose ghost appears to walk in far too many pavilions of other countries. He will not comment on what other counties are doing but one feels that he is worried that too many are nearer the Grace era than the space age of the seventies.

The Test and County Boards he believes could do with a shake-up, although they are an improvement on the old set-up at Lord's. However, those gentlemen can sleep on peacefully as he says there is enough work to keep him busy at Lancashire to have thoughts of tackling national problems.

One thing he does agree with is the present balance of three-day and one-day games. 'This is just right and there must be no further

Cedric Rhoades talking to West Indies skipper Gary Sobers; but for once
the chairman wasn't successful when he tried to get the world's No. 1 all-
rounder to sign for Lancashire.

increase of one-day games for this would lessen its appeal and destroy what we are trying to create.'

Even Rhoades finds that you can't win them all and one fight he has so far lost is to get women admitted to the Old Trafford pavilion. But with determination in every word he said: 'I will win it eventually. It will take time, possibly five years, but I'll do it.'

I don't doubt it, particularly when you consider that he started work as an office boy in a Manchester textile business and 16 years ago he took it over.

# Chapter 3

# Bond, the born battler
## by Brian Bearshaw

JACK BOND is acknowledged throughout first-class cricket as a shrewd, far-seeing captain. He is a thoroughly professional player, and it is widely recognised that he has played an enormous part in the resurgence of Lancashire. Yet less than four years ago there was a good chance that Bond, then 35 years old, would not be retained by the county.

However strong the chance was, Bond himself, at any rate, believed he might go, and he will tell you with a perfectly straight face that the only thing that saved him was being taken with the team to Cheltenham where a Sportsmen's Service was to be held on the Sunday and at which a Lancashire player was to read the lesson. And as a practising Methodist, Bond was a good choice. He was 12th man in the match at Cheltenham—and lesson reader, too—and 12th man in the following match at Worcester. But when the captain, Brian Statham, sent the injured and ill Geoff Pullar back to Old Trafford, Bond was brought into the team for the game against Essex at Chelmsford where he scored 64 and 37 in the 24-run victory.

If his Methodist devotions did save Bond, it was no more than he deserved. He and his family are regular churchgoers, he has even called his son Wesley, and he makes every effort to attend church in the morning before Sunday League games. And with the ups and downs, the heartaches and disappointments he has suffered, it was as well that he had this greater faith to support him.

Bond's début for Lancashire was against Surrey at Old Trafford towards the end of the 1955 season when he was 23 years old. The county's handbook the following year had these words of encourage-

Jack Bond is a skipper who leads by example—and here he gives a perfect demonstration of the off-drive.

28

ment for him: 'A very neat little right-hand bat who impressed on his second appearance.' Certainly, he could not have impressed on his first appearance where he batted No. 5, and failed to score in the first innings, although he improved noticeably in the second when he at least got off the mark—just. He was dispatched both times by Tony Lock, caught by Mickey Stewart first time, and then caught and bowled. Lock, incidentally, took 8–82 and 54–8 in this match to conduct Surrey safely to a seven-wicket win. No, not a dream début for Bond.

He played in the next match, too, when he impressed with his 'neatness', going in to bat with the total a magnificent 257–4 and scoring 25. Whatever he had done that day it would have needed a fabulous innings to follow centuries by Johnny Ikin and Cyril Washbrook. That was all Lancashire saw of Bond that year, one run in his first match, 25 in the second.

But that single acorn of his début match turned into a gigantic oak in 1961 when Bond scored 1,701 runs, including a brilliant century in 93 minutes against Sussex at Old Trafford. There was much more for the Year Book to get its teeth into the following year. 'Improved out of all recognition among the young players,' it said. And that at 29 years of age. . . . His peak came in 1962 when he hit five centuries and topped 2,000 runs, over 800 of them coming in June alone.

Bond really had arrived. He was Lancashire's established No. 3 batsman, a reliable and often punishing bat and if such progress could be maintained honours might well come his way. But in 1963, early in May, one ball from West Indian Wes Hall set the 31-year-old Bond back so far he never recovered. At least in figures he never again matched up to the sparkle he had produced in 1961 and 1962. The ball from Hall broke his wrist and although he later said he thought it had no effect on his batting he started the 1964 season badly and was dropped midway through it.

Lancashire unfortunately lost faith in this plucky batsman. Yet they were far from blessed with an abundance of talent. Their batting problems seemed incalculable. Nobody would have been surprised if Denis Law had been called up, yet the talented Bond could not hold his place. Lancashire persevered unreasonably with Gerry Knox, for example, who scored one century and one 50 in 45 visits to the wicket, but still Bond hung around, wondering if the confidence in him would be restored, and Lancashire would look at him again. Senior players wanted Bond in the side. They wanted his fight, his ability, his graft, and there is no question that he was an

30

infinitely better bat than many of the pretenders who were tried.

But it wasn't to be. In 1965 he was again dropped midway through the season and in 1966 and 1967 it was June before he got into the team. Speculation arose as to whether he would even be retained. But he was needed to read the lesson at Cheltenham, a job he did admirably. It was quite possible that this was Bond's last chance. It just had to be taken, and with Statham retiring and David Green being sacked, Lancashire turned, with a measure of reluctance it seemed, to the capable Bond.

Roy Collins, the former Lancashire all-rounder, reckons that many people still don't realise what a wonderful job Bond has done at Old Trafford. 'His true merit will only be seen when he retires and some poor chap has to follow,' he says.

Bond has taken his position as captain with due seriousness. He has always appreciated the dignity of his rank and the demands it makes upon him and he is nothing but courteous and friendly to the many people who want to see the captain of Lancashire. 'Strange though,' he said at the start of his second season. 'I've suddenly become a heck of a good after-dinner speaker.'

He has, too, with a dry wit and the ability to tell many a good cricket story. He is good to listen to and has his own definite opinions on cricket, the way to play it, run it, sell it. In other words Jack Bond is a professional. He thinks and thinks about the game, and while he isn't one to dwell too heavily on the day that has just gone, if it offered any lessons, then he is prepared to be taught and to use them to advantage in the future.

But he can be a worrier. In his first season as captain in 1968, I thought the many extra cares of captaincy seemed to be weighing him down on occasions. 'It's a hard game,' he said one day with feeling. He didn't sleep well for a time and on certain days would look weary, as if he badly needed a rest. But above all Bond is a fighter, and as a batsman he prefers the situations that make him battle for runs. He is usually seen at his best, not following a scoring spree when the bowling has been torn apart, but when his team are in trouble, when a player prepared to graft and fight, fight, fight, is called for.

This is a quality he has instilled into his team by example. And he hates to see a wicket thrown away wantonly. But for all this hardness, he is a philosophical player who believes that everything evens out. In one match against Nottinghamshire it was extremely doubtful whether he was out. 'Everything balances,' he said simply. 'Another day the benefit of the doubt will be mine.' This is why he believes that it is only the averages over a full season that are worth considering and why he fought to have them removed from the notice board in the Old Trafford pavilion when they started to appear there regularly during the season.

Bond has always been a team man, unselfish to a remarkable degree. And this, I believe, has been his strong suit in knitting the present side together. He plays for them and believes in them, and is prepared to put every one of the remaining 10 before himself. Personal success means absolutely nothing to Bond. If he scored 100 and Lancashire lost, he would be the unhappiest man in England. Let him bag a pair, but be on the winning side and his happiness overflows.

As with his fighting qualities, he has displayed his unselfishness by example. And I especially recall him in the match against Northamptonshire at Northampton in July 1968. Lancashire dismissed Northants for 218 and in front of a big crowd on a sunny Sunday, they looked to build up a useful lead. Four wickets had fallen for 106 when Bond went in to bat, and gradually, first with Farokh Engineer's help and then David Hughes, he turned the tide his own way.

Bond was in splendid form and took control of the innings. He scored all round the wicket, but was particularly punishing on the on side, two or three times picking the ball up beautifully over mid-wicket for towering fours that were only feet away from being sixes. Each time he banged his bat on the ground in mock anger. But it didn't seem to matter. A century looked a formality. But when only seven away from his first hundred in three years he declared so that his bowlers could have a half-hour fling at the Northants batsmen. The crowd recognised the sacrifice he had made and rose to applaud as he left the field. It was a fine gesture and it paid off. Northants lost three wickets for 11 runs that evening, were all out for 62 on the Monday morning, and Lancashire walked off with a 10-wicket win.

His unselfishness had not been anywhere near so evident to spectators the previous year when he was in the 12 Lancashire took to Wellingborough . . . and suggested to Brian Statham on the field before the match that he be left out in favour of a bowler. Bond thought another specialist bowler was needed, a shrewd opinion as it turned out with Lancashire winning by five wickets with three minutes to spare.

He has endeared himself to the members of his team and is highly respected. It showed through for me in the Sunday League match at Bournemouth last season when he went into bat for the final over

It's a sunshine life for Jack Bond. For after playing cricket in the summer he spent the winter helping other people to plan their holidays in the sun by working for a Manchester travel agent.

with the score 200–5. He was not interested in being not out for himself and kept on running and running off the last ball of the allotted 40 overs so that he was easily run out. Barry Wood stood in the players' enclosure at the side of the pavilion, shook his head and said simply, and almost with affection: 'Aaay, captain.'

Have no doubts, Lancashire cricket means more to Bond than any words of mine can express. The players are in no doubt. Last season when the match against Glamorgan at Blackpool was over it was pointed out that the leaders in the bowlers' race for 100 wickets and a Ford Capri were Peter Lever and Tony Buss . . . and they were rivals in the next match at Hove. 'Captain,' said Lever to Bond. 'I've had a brainwave how to win this Capri in the next match,' he said with obvious jest. Joke or no, Bond quickly had everybody in no doubt as to what he thought. 'What's it to be?' he asked. 'The championship or the car?' It was an unnecessary question, but he felt it had to be said.

His strong personality is showing through Lancashire cricket and when they are in the field, a spectator would have to be both blind and deaf not to realise who was skipper. Tactically there are few to match him and he changes his field often to suit mood and batsmen. His fieldsmen are kept on their toes and his eager close-set eyes are forever roaming the field, making sure every man is in his right position and doing his duty.

The lighter side of the man shows through, too. In the Sunday League match against Derbyshire at Buxton last season a persistent dog caused a few headaches by doing two laps of honour and refusing to leave the field. Bond gave everybody at the ground and the hundreds of thousands at home watching television a laugh by grabbing a stump, holding it like a spear and chasing the dog. And in case any humourless souls think he had evil intent let me assure them he has a dog of his own.

Bond is a man with a keen sense of humour and while he takes cricket extremely seriously, he never misses the opportunity for a laugh. At Tunbridge Wells in 1969, the Kent crowd, while wincing frequently, were treated to an exciting exhibition of batting from Farokh Engineer, from India, and David Bailey, from Durham. In under two hours they hit 144 glorious runs, but a partial collapse left Lancashire 196–5 at tea with the position needing consolidation once more. Bond, from Bolton, and David Hughes, from Newton-le-Willows, were the not out batsmen. When the time came for them to leave the dressing-room, Bond reached for his cap. 'Come on David,' he said. 'Let's restore a bit of Lancashire sanity to the situation.' Lancashire had to build again. In half an hour they got 10. . . .

I once asked Bond about the fast bowlers he faced during his career. Wes Hall came up of course. So did Freddie Trueman and Frank Tyson. Bond once faced 'Typhoon' Tyson at Blackpool and was hit on the chest by a ball from him. 'They had to get me a glass of water to bring me round properly,' he said. The next ball was a half volley and a grateful Bond hit it into the covers for two. 'I was a fool,' he said. 'A great fool. I should have hit it for one.'

The tension can be terrific for any successful team, especially as the season draws on and they are in line for honours. And while it is so wonderful to see a title clinched, it is good, too, to see players relax, to watch the tension roll off them. The day after Lancashire clinched the Sunday League title in 1969 by beating Warwickshire at Nuneaton, they continued their county match against them at Edgbaston on the Monday.

Champagne time for Jack Bond at a civic reception given by Manchester City Council in honour of Lancashire's double success in 1970. Pouring the champagne is the Lord Mayor, Councillor William Downward and also in the picture are, left to right, Barry Wood, David Bailey, Clive Lloyd, Johnny Sullivan and Farokh Engineer.

In the morning Lancashire managed to avoid following on and Warwickshire batted again in the afternoon with a lead of 116. After tea I left the Press Box and stood with the small crowd opposite the pavilion, directly behind Bond fielding in his usual position in the gully. He looked round checking his field before the start of one over and looked over in my direction. There was no fieldsman there, but Bond waved his hand to get the 'ghost' to move. I moved 25 yards to my right until Bond was satisfied and raised his hand for me to stop. John Jameson was batting and looked amazed at Bond.

When the over was completed, Bond changed ends and waved me back 25 yards to where I had been. Jameson leaned on his bat, his hand on one hip, looking for the invisible fielder. It was the end of the season, the last championship match, and the tension had gone. I looked at Bond. Aaay, captain. . . .

*Chapter 4*

# John Player League champions again

*by Vernon Addison*

ON 30 August 1970, the *Sunday Times* asked in a headline uncharacteristically big and black: 'Is cricket dead?'

If cricket was dead on that day then round Lancashire they were making a 'reet good do' of the funeral.

While many would still be reading what seemed to be the last rites on the national game, almost 40,000 cricket followers were en route to Old Trafford to see Lancashire retain the John Player League title in the second year of its competition. Exactly 27,549 of them gained admission legally to the match with Yorkshire; several hundred more displayed misplaced, but understandable, ingenuity to enter illegally; while thousands of the law-abiding hurriedly returned home offering prayers that the TV set hadn't broken down.

All this made it even more incredible that what the *Sunday Times* presented as a serious survey of the undoubted problems facing the national game—it was elevated from the sports section to the main feature pages—failed even once to mention Lancashire where the game has proved there is a second life.

Perhaps this was because one-day cricket was disparagingly dismissed as 'candyfloss' and, of course, the reincarnation of Lancashire cricket started with the Sunday League. All too often the phenomena of one-day cricket has been begrudgingly acknowledged as an illegitimate son who turns out to be brilliant.

Some players have not helped, openly calling it 'comic cricket'. Others, rather like the man in the advert who says he's only here for the beer, say they are only there for the spectators. But how can you

Jack Simmons, who struck a great blow for spin bowlers in one-day cricket by coming third in the national John Player League averages in 1970.

ignore the demands of the public?

The time surely has come when the one-day game is taken as seriously as the three-day county championship. After all, no one has caught the plague from playing it!

It is appropriate that Lancashire were the first side to appreciate the Sunday League for league cricket has been a feature of the county's sporting life. Since the war alone it has attracted such great names as Gary Sobers, Ray Lindwall, Sir Frank Worrell, Eddie Barlow, Charlie Griffith, Sonny Ramadhin, Wes Hall, Bobby Simpson, Everton Weekes, Clive Walcott, Alf Valentine and Basil D'Oliveira—an off-the-cuff list which is sure to give offence by omission.

Simpson, who went on to captain Australia, and D'Oliveira who bridged the enormous gap from underprivileged Coloured cricket in South Africa to the Test arena, have often said that the League was their making. They—and many others—have described the league game as the best in the world with so much action compressed into a few hours. What's good enough for these world stars on Saturday must surely be good enough for all our counties on Sunday.

Certainly Lancashire cannot be accused of cheapening the game when Harry Pilling became the first player in any county to score 1,000 runs in the Sunday League. At 5 ft. $2\frac{1}{2}$ ins. the smallest player in the game today, he can hardly be described as a muck-or-nettles slogger.

Lancashire, too, have proved that one-day cricket is no knackers yard for spinners for Jack Simmons was third in the League averages with 26 wickets in 98.5 overs for a return of 14.07 ,while the left-handed David Hughes was one place behind with 24 wickets in 83.4 overs for an analysis of 14.50. Leg spinners, anyway, have long been near-museum pieces in the three day game despite the importation of Intikhab and Mushtaq to join Robin Hobbs and Harry Latchman.

The purists criticise the scarcity of slip fielders, but they miss the point for, with the accent switched to out-cricket, Lancashire's work in the field has played nearly as big a part in bringing back the spectacle to the game as the big-hitting of Clive Lloyd, Farokh Engineer and Johnny Sullivan.

Another sacred cow that has been put to the slaughter are averages. They are particularly meaningless to middle-order batsmen and have been superseded in importance by team-work. No mourners, please, for averages bear a heavy burden of guilt for putting county cricket into a deep sleep.

The only valid complaints with the Player League are the curbing

A big hit by John Sullivan which shows why he was so ideally suited for the John Player League where he highlighted his performances with a magnificent 56 not out in the title-clinching game with Yorkshire.

The kind of scene they said was a thing of the past in cricket. Harry Pilling forces his way through the huge crowd after guiding Lancashire to victory over Yorkshire on August 30, 1970, a win which gave them the John Player League for the second year on the run. Note how many youngsters there are in this section of the Old Trafford crowd which, with gate-crashers, must have topped 30,000 that day.

of bowlers run-ups which tends to bring the genuine quickies down to the level of the run-of-the-mill medium-pace trundlers and the reduction of weather-hit games to as little as ten overs each. While the enthusiasm to stage a game of sorts is to be admired, anything less than 20 overs a side is fit only for the Whitehall Theatre.

There will always be a place for the three-day game, which is the only training ground for Test matches but the John Player League and the Gillette Cup are worthy of equal status with their much elder brother for they have brought back entertainment and excitement to cricket.

It all made for an unforgettable day on 30 August when those planners who messed about with our traditional Bank Holidays proved that they knew a thing or two after all. For what better way for Lancashire to win a title than on the last match against the old enemy on a glorious Bank Holiday?

In the end the occasion was greater than the match for only in the early stages of the Yorkshire innings did they give the massed army of Red Rose followers any palpitations. Then Geoff Boycott played a magnificent innings, but like the poetic sea captain, he alone stayed at the bridge, hitting 81 out of 165 as Yorkshire capitulated from 111–2.

In this form Boycott's dismissal just had to be spectacular—and from Lancashire's point of view it could not have been more appropriate. For Jack Bond's diving catch, the first of three wickets in four balls by Ken Shuttleworth, typified their cricket all season. It typified, too, Bond's leadership by example.

The rest of Yorkshire's batting was an obituary. Doug Padgett and John Woodford were run out by the sort of distances which leave room for recrimination long afterwards. Then Yorkshire sons have been disowned for less than the cross-bat shots of Test players Phil Sharpe and Jackie Hampshire, who went identically lbw to David Hughes, and the limp fishing shot of Richard Hutton, which could only result in a catch behind the wicket. After that the least Hutton can do is change his famous surname by deed poll.

It was left to Jack Simmons, one of the less spectacular members of the Lancs team, to earn himself a rare share of the limelight by ending their innings with two wickets in two balls. So he had all winter to contemplate a place in the Guinness Book of Records, for a wicket with his first Sunday League ball next season must surely give him the longest hat-trick in the game's history.

When Lancashire batted, Pilling was so obviously there for the duration that victory was just a matter of time. Perhaps there was an air of unusual tension, but when they slipped behind the clock Clive Lloyd gave a touch of the accelerator with 20—four boundaries—in ten minutes. Then John Sullivan opened up the throttle to the full, highlighting his unbeaten 56 with a straight driven six off Richard Hutton and seven fours. With the Old Trafford Kop in full voice, Pilling's 55th run brought Lancashire victory by the comprehensive margin of seven wickets and 25 balls.

Yorkshire, however, never concede defeat until the situation is beyond even schoolboy fiction and off that winning shot they tried to run out Harry. When the wicket was broken the chanting crowd had already gone over the top and had Pilling been out of his ground it is interesting to ponder what an umpire would have done. It could have affected only the margin of victory and clearing the ground was well-nigh impossible. Perhaps his only course would be to keep the truth for his Maker or his memoirs, whichever he valued more highly.

So Lancashire, whose average scoring rate for the season was over five runs an over, were champions again having lost only two rain-interfered games, the kind for which you need to be a cross between a mathematical genius and legal expert to understand the points scoring system.

That's a record to be taken seriously.

A picture which tells a story. Fielding has been a top priority in the Jack Bond era—with the skipper setting the example. Here he shows the way with a great diving catch to dismiss Geoff Boycott in the final Player League match of 1970.

The title hat-trick. On the left is the John Player League double. Below
Jack Bond receives the £1,000 cheque from Mr. R. A. Garrett, chairman
of John Player's, after their 1969 success while above Bond tries to balance
the trophy on his head after they won it again in 1970. With him are
Peter Lever, Jack Simmons and Barry Wood. On the right Bond and Farokh
Engineer hoist the Gillette Cup to show their delighted fans at Lord's last
year. Around them are David Hughes, Clive Lloyd, Peter Lever and Barry
Wood.

# Chapter 5

# Lord of Lord's
*by Brian Bearshaw*

I CAN still feel my stomach churning when I think back to Clive Lloyd being brilliantly caught by Geoff Greenidge running in front of the Mound Stand at Lord's on 5 September when Lancashire took part in their first Gillette Cup Final.

It wasn't that I hadn't faith in the remaining seven wickets getting the 99 runs needed for victory over Sussex. Goodness knows, there was plenty of batting still to come with Harry Pilling still there, Johnny Sullivan ready to come out, by Farokh Engineer, Jack Bond and Jack Simmons, who had hit 100 against Sussex at Hove only a month before.

Perhaps we Lancastrians had spent too long before the match weighing up both teams' weaknesses and strengths, looking admiringly at Lancashire's stirring efforts in the field, and knowing that in Clive we had one of the handful of men in the country who can win you a match with one hour's hectic batting.

Our appetites had been whetted by that effortless six he had just struck. Here we go, we thought. Now for the onslaught. Instead of which Clive, his head bowed and pushed forward, was setting his long strides off in the direction of the pavilion.

The tension was now at its greatest. The tension that soon rises from your stomach to your throat and you know if it isn't eased soon, you'll be ready to be sick with anybody. But of course Lancashire would still win. Wasn't this what we had assured ourselves back in May when Lancashire went to Bristol to take on Gloucestershire, the team many fancied to go a long way in this competition.

Luckily Lancashire had won a bye into the second round. They had avoided that terrible day of 25 April when only one of five first-round matches scheduled that day could take place. The competition suddenly became a lottery as Yorkshire found in the following two days when they played in the snow and were all out for 76 to Surrey.

The Gillette Cup has become too important for clubs to subject themselves to the terrors of an English April when players have had hardly any practice—in some cases no practice at all—in the 'middle'. Soccer has discovered that the best time for its knock-out competition is later in the season when clubs are fully into their stride and when supporters of languishing clubs look for the FA Cup to give them a much-needed boost. Cricket could do worse than follow the example of football by letting the Minor Counties take part in an early-season eliminating contest to find those who will join the first-class counties in the opening round some time in June. And there's no doubt that 'gates' will be much, much better at this time than in April.

Warwickshire, one of the Gillette Cup strong teams, were beaten by Nottinghamshire at 8 p.m. in near darkness and in a steady drizzle, and by the end of the first round, Warwickshire and Yorkshire, alas, were no more.

The second round was held in vastly more pleasant conditions on 30 May when Lancashire went to Bristol and Sussex took on Essex at Chelmsford. Mike Buss, Sussex's reliable opening bat scored 72, took 2–25 in 12 overs and was the man of the match as Essex were beaten by four wickets.

Lancashire, meanwhile, made a tremendous start against Gloucestershire with an opening stand of 63 between David Lloyd and Barry Wood, followed by a third-wicket stand of 66 as they raced to a formidable 278–2 from the alloted 60 overs.

Nobody gave Gloucestershire much chance. After all, the highest score by a team batting second in the eight years of the competition had been 271 by Nottinghamshire against Gloucestershire in 1968. There was a chance of Gloucestershire getting there, of course, but not much.

At least that's what we thought. David Green, the former Lancashire opening batsman, and one of the best strikers of the ball in the game, was opening for Gloucestershire. Jack Bond wasted no time in setting a ring of fieldsmen to Green. And the closest man to the bat in the field was Bond himself, in the gully. 'Why don't you clear off as well?' Green said to him. 'No,' said Bond. 'I'm staying here to catch you off Peter.' In Peter Lever's following over, Green flashed mightily at the ball, Bond picked it up and Green departed . . .

c Bond b Lever 9.

But then came a second-wicket stand between Ron Nicholls, the man of the match for his inspiring 75, and Mike Bissex, and when Gloucestershire moved to 141-2, Lancashire looked to be losing their grip. Jack Simmons, however, took three cheap wickets, dismissing David Shepherd, Wycliffe Phillips and Mike Proctor to rip the heart out of the team. But then came a frustrating eighth-wicket stand between David Allen and David Smith that added 51 and sent Gloucestershire's hopes soaring again. With three overs to go 31 more runs were needed for victory. Recalling the situation some weeks later Johnny Sullivan, the sixth bowler Lancashire had tried, remembered looking at the scoreboard at this point. 'Hey skipper,' he said to Bond. 'They want 31 in three overs . . . and I'm bowling two of 'em!'

But he need have had no fears. When the last man fell with 11 balls still to go, Gloucestershire were all out for 251, 27 behind.

Sussex were away again for the third round on 8 July, but pulled off a remarkably good win at Canterbury when they beat Kent by 47 runs, Tony Greig being an easy man of the match choice for adjudicator Freddie Brown by following his 54 runs with five wickets for 42 runs.

Lancashire, however, were at Old Trafford, facing Hampshire, the team they had demolished in the Sunday League at Bournemouth two weeks before. Hampshire made a dreadful start. Keith Wheatley was run out before he had faced a ball, a victim of a fine throw from the boundary edge by Harry Pilling, and in no time at all their first three batsmen were out for 10 runs.

Roy Marshall and Danny Livingstone, with a fourth-wicket stand of 72, and Alan Castell and Butch White, sharing in a stand of 45 for the last wicket, lifted Hampshire to 142. Lancashire started almost as badly as Hampshire by losing Engineer and Pilling for only 12, but Barry Wood, partnered first by Clive Lloyd and then Johnny Sullivan, steered Lancashire to an easy five-wicket win after only 35.3 overs. Peter Lever's 5-30 in his 12 overs won him the individual award from adjudicator Don Kenyon, but he could have been only a nose ahead of Wood, who used this innings as the springboard for his exceptionally fine batting in the last two months of the season that brought him over 1,000 runs.

And so to the semi-finals two weeks later. This was Sussex's sixth semi-final in eight years and their tremendously-exciting win over Surrey at the Oval took them to the final for the fourth time, a record that utterly justified their claim to be the Kings of Gillette cricket. With one ball to go, Sussex were 194–8 in reply to Surrey's 196 all out. John Snow struck; it looked only a single but Intikhab misfielded and they ran two. So Sussex won by having two wickets in hand when the scores were level after 60 overs.

For Lancashire this was their fourth semi-final. Would they succeed this time where they had failed on every previous occasion, losing to Worcestershire by nine wickets in 1963, to Warwickshire by 85 runs in 1964, and to Somerset—yes Somerset—by 100 runs in 1967?

They travelled to Taunton from Derby, having just lost their first championship match of the season, a crushing 10-wicket defeat from Derbyshire who had scored 468–5 in their first innings. A beating hurts at the best of times, and it certainly rankled particularly with Wood. What is it about Yorkshiremen that makes them even more upset by defeat than Lancastrians? And a Yorkshireman playing for Lancashire at that. . . .

When Derbyshire batted a second time they needed only seven to win. Wood had already packed his bag and even stowed it away in his car for the journey to Taunton. With Lancashire's last wicket ready to fall he dashed outside, rescued his tackle, ran back to the dressing-room and shouted to Ken Shuttleworth, who had been injured and was 12th man: 'And you'd better get changed as well. I just might go lame.' And when Engineer, Pilling and Frank Hayes jostled for the right to bowl the deciding overs with Johnny Sullivan buckling on the pads ready to keep wicket, Wood growled: 'Give 'em nowt. Put proper bowlers on. We might get a wicket.'

In this frame of mind, he went to Taunton, took 3–35 and hit 31 runs and became man of the match in Lancashire's thrilling four-wicket win. The day was beautiful, and Somerset were rewarded with the biggest crowd in years, the largest, in fact, since the great 1948 Australian side were visitors.

Somerset opener Roy Virgin, who had hit 52 and 103 in his two other Gillette Cup innings of the season, continued to sing the same song against Lancashire and scored an excellent 65 before he was bowled by David Hughes. This proved the turning point of the Somerset innings. One minute they were 119–1 with plenty of overs left and threatening to rip Lancashire to pieces. But with Virgin gone, Lancashire took a firm hold and despite a temporary hold-up in which 31 runs were added for the eighth wicket, they dismissed Somerset for 207.

Lancashire lost half their wickets, including that of Clive Lloyd in reaching 130 and for a time our hearts faltered while Sullivan and

Bond took control once more to steer Lancashire to their first Gillette Cup Final.

Oh, it was good to be at Lord's that warm September day. It's good to be at Lord's any old time, but this was even more satisfying, more gratifying even than winning the Sunday League in its first two seasons. The crowds swarmed around Lord's like ants, gaily-dressed ants, well-provided-for ants with plenty of tinned and bottled beer—there's a fortune waiting for the man who invents instant beer—to supplement the picnic lunches and teas through the game that was due to last eight hours.

There were red roses in abundance and one man had even made a chain of them to go round his trilby. A rich, red rose is a lovely sight. It was thrilling to see so many again, all freshly picked, still looking crisp and bright.

Lancashire's fielding, as ever, was crisp and bright, too. They were like tigers, pouncing on anything that moved, and pounding after every ball with a rare determination. Clive Lloyd prowled around mid-wicket and cover and his mere presence saved Lancashire a fistful of runs as the Sussex batsmen bowed to the threat of one of the world's finest fielders.

The morning session of two hours was strangely similar to that of an average championship match. Both sides probed, looking, waiting for the opening that never came. Peter Lever and Ken Shuttleworth bowled magnificently and gave nothing away, backed up by the fielding which Arthur Gilligan later described as the finest he had ever seen.

Mike Buss threatened briefly to take charge. In five previous innings against Lancashire in August he had scored 228 runs, including 51 and a hurricane 91 in the championship match at Hove. Today he scored 42 before he was third out at 68, 42 delightful runs with the well-timed strokes of a man in form. The 20 minutes after lunch were obviously to be the vital ones for both teams. It was here that either Lancashire or Sussex would take charge, it was here where the match could be won or lost.

For a few minutes Jim Parks, who had played in both Sussex's Cup Final wins of 1963 and 1964, threatened to take command. Then David Hughes struck. He removed Parks, Tony Greig and Peter Graves and three important wickets had fallen for 36 runs. While the wickets of Mike Buss and Parks were probably the most important from Lancashire's point of view, the one that stays in my mind is that of Graves. Graves, described by Roy Marshall as one of the three most promising young batsmen in the country, looked to give himself fully a yard as he backed off to make room for a vicious-looking cut. He bent at the knees, there was plenty of power in the stroke, but he didn't make contact and was bowled.

Sussex now could not break free and at the end of 60 overs they were 184–9, a total widely considered to be far too modest for Lancashire's batting, which has so much depth these days. The last three Sussex wickets fell to run outs, the results of fine fielding by Clive Lloyd, Lever and Pilling.

Victory, while no formality, would certainly be easy. In the Press Box Denis Compton forecast victory by 5.30 with plenty of wickets in hand. Ted Dexter, the Sussex captain in their winning years, kept quiet. Writer and broadcaster John Arlott pointed out that when Sussex won the first Final seven years before they did it with a poor-looking total of 168. Now that was something I hadn't noticed. I quickly looked at the other six finals and found much more comfort in the final of 1968 when Sussex batted first, scored 214–7, and then lost by four wickets to Warwickshire.

Lancashire were soon in trouble when openers David Lloyd and Wood were dismissed for 37 runs, and then, as I say, the tension really mounted when Clive, darn him, loped his way back to the pavilion. Sullivan added 15, but when he was caught at the wicket Lancashire needed 72 more to win and the rate was about four an over. Another wicket or two and Sussex really were in the game. But they weren't to get another wicket. Pilling refused to move. He it was who guided Lancashire home, calmly, steadily, ignoring the storm that threatened momentarily to break. He picked up runs quietly, unobtrusively, finding the gaps and exploiting them, and occasionally letting go a full-blooded stroke, like the cover drive he unleashed that looked likely to bounce all the way back from the boundary.

At the end of every over, and once or twice during them, he chatted to his partner, Engineer. Pilling was directing the operation, that was for sure. The flamboyant Engineer, who can at times be so reckless, played magnificently and refused to be tempted into a rush of rash strokes.

'I kept telling him we had plenty of time, there was no hurry,' said Pilling after. "Can I hit Greig over the top now?" he asked me. "You do that and I'll crack you one," I told him. He only had one rush of blood and that was when he lapped Snow for four off his middle stump. It was a fantastic shot.'

In the end victory came easily. Lancashire coasted in by six wickets with 4.5 overs left. Pilling was duly named man of the

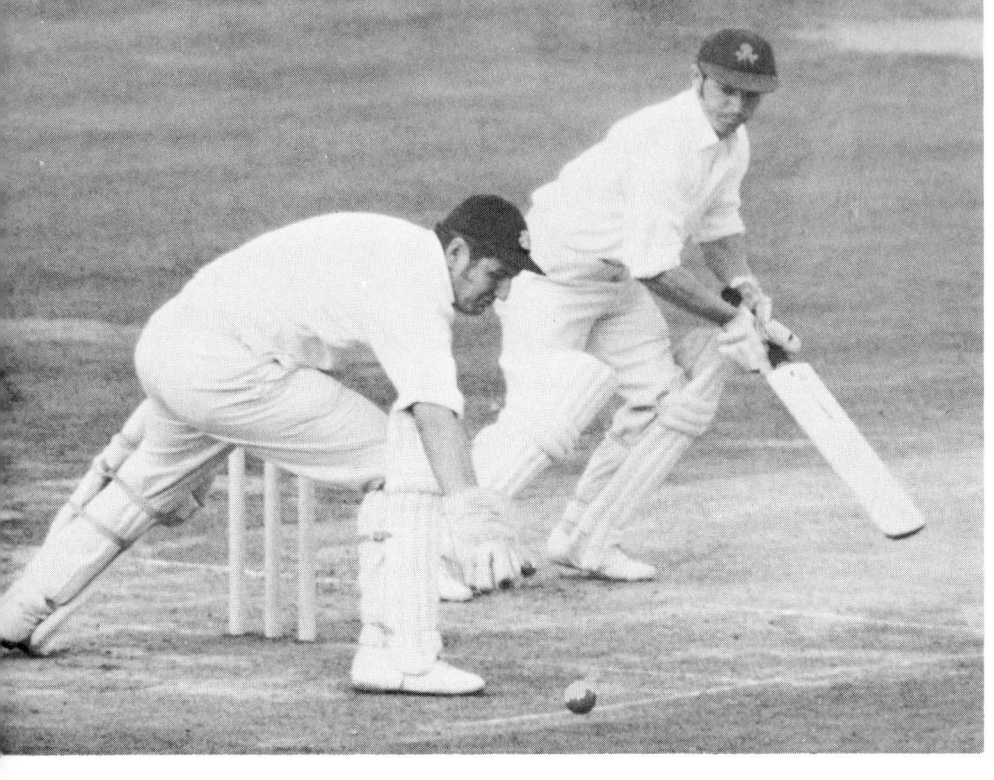

Harry Pilling, the man of the match in the Gillette Cup Final cuts Mike Buss past Sussex wicket-keeper Jim Parks.

match and you would have thought Lancashire had lost if you had seen all the tears in the dressing-room afterwards. And one of the nicest parts of a splendid day was when Engineer quietly thanked Pilling for his help.

I wondered about Sussex, and with that wonderful insight that comes to everybody after the happening, considered Mike Griffith's tactics in the last half-hour. He used only five bowlers altogether, holding back John Snow and Tony Buss for the last fling that never paid off. As Lancashire were moving forward and as Sussex sunk with every run I looked at Dexter and wondered what he would have done. He probably would not have let the established pattern continue. He would have tried to break the batsmen's concentration. Would he have played to Engineer's impetuosity, maybe even allowed

Barry Wood cracks one to the off in the Gillette Cup final.

42-year-old Ken Suttle an over or two of slow left hand mysteries to tempt and taunt.

It's delightful to sit back weeks later and wonder what might have happened if this had been done or that had been changed. But it's even more delightful to look back on Lancashire's victory. I'll relish that for years to come.

One aspect at Lord's did disappoint me. And that was the crowd. For such a large audience, there was very little atmosphere, not enough enthusiasm and cheering. Things did warm up a little late in the afternoon as Lancashire strode on and the alcoholic flush took hold of a few.

Was it that the game only rarely touched the heights expected of such a showpiece? Were Lancashire too thorough? They were almost mechanically perfect, grinding on to an expected end.

# GILLETTE CUP FINAL SCOREBOARD

| | |
|---|---|
| M. A. Buss b Simmons | 42 |
| G. A. Greenidge b Shuttleworth | 2 |
| R. J. Langridge c D. Lloyd b C. Lloyd | 9 |
| J. M. Parks b Hughes | 34 |
| A. W. Greig b Hughes | 15 |
| P. J. Graves b Hughes | 16 |
| K. G. Suttle run out | 23 |
| M. G. Griffith run out | 10 |
| A. Buss not out | 13 |
| J. A. Snow run out | 0 |
| J. S. Spencer not out | 5 |
| Extras (b 4, lb 6, nb 5) | 15 |
| Total (9 wkts. inns. closed) | 184 |

*Fall of wickets:* 1–7, 2–34, 3–68, 4–113, 5–114, 6–149, 7–161, 8–164, 9–173.

*Bowling:* Shuttleworth 12–0–31–1, Lever 12–3–31–0, C. Lloyd 12–1–46–1, Simmons 12–1–30–1, Hughes 12–2–31–3.

LANCASHIRE

| | |
|---|---|
| B. Wood c Snow b M. Buss | 22 |
| D. Lloyd b Spencer | 12 |
| H. Pilling not out | 70 |
| C. H. Lloyd c Greenidge b M. Buss | 29 |
| J. Sullivan c Parks b Greig | 15 |
| F. M. Engineer not out | 31 |
| Extras (lb 5, nb 1) | 6 |
| Total (4 wkts. 55.1 overs) | 185 |

*Fall of wickets:* 1–33, 2–37, 3–86, 4–113.

*Did not bat:* J. D. Bond, D. P. Hughes, J. Simmons, K. Shuttleworth, P. Lever.

*Bowling:* Snow 12–2–31–0, A. Buss 10.1–1–31–0, Spencer 11–1–40–1, M. Buss 12–2–34–2, Greig 10–0–43–1.

*Umpires:* C. S. Elliott and A. E. Fagg.

# BEST OF SEASON
## Performances and Awards 1970

## Batting: **Clive Lloyd**

**Top Scorer**

163 v Kent at Dartford

**Fastest 100**

100 in 74 balls v Somerset in Sunday League at Southport on July 12. Third fastest in country.

## Bowling: **David Hughes**

7 for 24 v Oxford University at Oxford.

### **Peter Lever**

7 for 83 for England v Rest of the World at the Oval, August 15.

**Harry Pilling**
v Sussex, Final. 70 Not Out.

**Barry Wood**
v Somerset, Semi-Final. Took 3-35, Scored 31.

## Gillette Cup
### Man Of The Match

**3 in year**

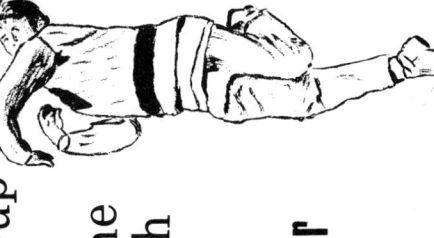

### **Peter Lever**
v Hampshire second round Took 5-30.

## Catches: **Farokh Engineer**

**Six in one innings**

Wicket-Keeper v Surrey at the Oval.

# Chapter 6

# The title that got away
*by John Kay*
(*Manchester Evening News*)

LANCASHIRE's success in the John Player League and Gillette Cup in 1970 has tended, not unnaturally, to overshadow the county championships. Yet this must not obscure some magnificent team and individual performances in the three day game where they finished a creditable third.

Barry Wood had his best season; Harry Pilling proved once again his consistency; Clive Lloyd electrified the crowds; Frank Hayes exploded on the scene; Peter Lever and Ken Shuttleworth gained their first caps and were further rewarded with selection for Australia; David Hughes had his career best figures and was the county's leading wicket-taker while Farokh Engineer continually made seemingly safe shots into catches.

In the end their failure to add the championship to the other two trophies was due to that old sporting handicap of fighting on too many fronts. The strains of the Sunday League programme certainly had its effect, especially on a Monday with a not unexpected 'wind down' from the excitement and demands of the previous day. This feeling was accentuated by the sudden loss of atmosphere, playing in front of 10,000 people one day and less than 2,000 the next.

No one better symbolised the fighting spirit of this new Lancashire than Barry Wood, one of the long list of exiled Yorkshiremen in first-class cricket.

He started by going up to Oxford and taking a century off the University attack. Then came the innings that he had waited for, his first hundred against his old county in the May 'Roses' match at Headingley. What a glorious touch he brought to it, reaching

56

three figures by driving Don Wilson for six. He hit another six, too, and 14 other boundaries in an innings of almost four hours.

This knock was not only the morale-booster he needed but it played a big part in lifting the team's inferiority complex that had tended to overshadow their championship cricket for years.

Helped by a sound 64 from David Lloyd, the opening stand of 151 was the cornerstone of their first victory in Yorkshire for ten years and by the convincing margin of ten wickets. Oddly enough the last win in Yorkshire in 1960 was also by ten wickets.

From then on Wood went from strength to strength. He wrote himself an unusual record by becoming the first Yorkshireman to hit centuries in both Roses matches for Lancashire, again reaching three figures with a six off Don Wilson. This innings also made him a member of an elite club for he was only the fifth Lancashire player to hit two centuries in a season against the old enemy. The others were A. C. MacLaren 1899, Cyril Washbrook 1948, Geoff Pullar 1959 and Jack Bond 1962. Wood also took hundreds off Sussex and Notts and was dismissed for 99 against Middlesex. He was the side's top run-getter with 1,457 from 44 first class innings, collected 31 wickets to top the bowling averages at 19.38 and held 15 catches.

Twice he dismissed the great Gary Sobers during one memorable weekend at Old Trafford and at Taunton he won the Gillette cup semi-final man of the match award. He was so obviously happy at his work that he was the life and soul of a merry Lancashire contingent and nowhere was this more evident than in the champagne celebration at Taunton where his rendering of 'Ilkley Moor 'Baht 'At' was unforgettable.

Wood and David Lloyd ranked with Kent's Brian Luckhurst and Mike Denness as the most consistent opening pair last season, yet skipper Jack Bond feels that there is something holding back the modest left-handed Lloyd. To show this talented player that the world was his for the asking Bond stood down for the match with Cambridge University and successfully pleaded for Lloyd to take charge. Time alone will tell if Bond's imaginative plan will work but Lloyd, whether he appreciates it or not, has the ability to open for England. He plays straight, pushing forward or going back, and places the ball with a delicate ease that comes from perfect timing. Although he missed several matches in the middle of the season with a back complaint he totalled 1,039 runs from 39 innings, being much more impressive in the closing weeks when the back trouble cleared and his determination to succeed mounted rapidly.

Once again Harry Pilling played the sheet anchor role to perfection. The smallest player in the game Lancashire regard Pilling as the 'Little Master' and 1,315 runs for an average of 38.67 represented another great season's work. He had one glorious fling in mid season, hitting four centuries in eight days including one in each innings against Warwickshire at Old Trafford.

Pilling hit up a trememdous understanding with Clive Lloyd and down in Gravesend I am sure they are still talking about their third wicket stand of 231 runs early in the season. Pilling's timing and ability to place the ball was in marked contrast to the furious hitting of the tall Lloyd but there was no finer sight last summer than these two on the rampage. Running between the wickets might have presented a problem for batsmen of such differing builds but never once did Pilling or Lloyd make a mistake in this respect. For Pilling it often meant a feverish dash while his long-striding partner strolled home at the other end but they developed such an understanding, often scorning calls and substituting a nod of the head, that Pilling confessed his only concern was that Lloyd 'might bloody well tread on me'!

Lloyd's contribution can never be assessed in figures. He topped the averages with 46.26 from a total of 1,203 runs but the magic of the West Indies left-hander's cricket lay in his ability to rouse the crowd. No innings from Lloyd was ever dull. He could hit one delivery out of the ground for six and edge the next cheekily between the slips. It was said that Clive was suspect early in an innings. One or two fast bowlers tempted him to hook and get caught on the boundary but as the summer wore on he learned to discipline himself and was a much harder opponent for sacrificing his favourite shot. His medium-paced seamers were often used as front line support for Peter Lever and Ken Shuttleworth and he was always liable to break through. Even if he did get a duck and take none for plenty—which was rare—he was worth watching for his fielding which often bordered on the miraculous. Some of his catches at cover beggared description and his picking up and throwing saw batsmen regularly stranded.

So there you see the backbone of the side, the first four batsmen all topped 1,000 runs while skipper Bond, Frank Hayes and Farokh Engineer each scored more than 700 runs.

Hayes was the batting discovery of the summer although he would never make that assertion himself. He proved himself a stylish stroke-player and a powerful hitter, producing a temperament to match his skills. Frank started his championship career with 94 against Middle-sex at Old Trafford and a few days later he got himself stumped for

This is the style that earned Lancashire's opening bowlers, Peter Lever, left, and Ken Shuttleworth their first Test caps last summer.

99 . . . sportingly putting the needs of his side in front of his own personal accomplishments. In 22 first class innings Hayes hit 719 runs and also took over the vital first slip position with promise.

59

Skipper Bond certainly had an overflow of batting riches and it became a tricky business deciding between Hayes, Ken Snellgrove and Johnny Sullivan for the final batting position as the championship programme neared its exciting end. Bond cast his vote for Hayes over the three-day distance and was undoubtedly right for Snellgrove and Sullivan were better equipped for the over-limited games.

Even with the absence of Clive Lloyd in all five matches for the Rest of the World against England, and Engineer in two of them, Lancashire fielded a batting line-up better than probably all counties except the eventual champions, Kent.

The spirit of the side was perfectly shown in the way that Sullivan, a capped player, cheerfully accepted promotion and relegation. A hard-hitting batsman, his seamers often confounded the best of batsmen and his contribution was 669 runs in 32 knocks, 22 wickets and 18 catches. It is no secret that he is on the wanted list of several counties who have noted his absences from the team. But this loyal and very popular player says: 'Great things are happening in Lancashire cricket these days—and I want to be part of them.'

Another batsman wanted elsewhere but valued too highly for Lancashire to contemplate releasing is Ken Snellgrove, talented hitter and ace fieldsman, who remains the man to put the pressure on the batsmen who waver. One of these days he will step up to plug a gap and do the job so well he will prove indispensable. As it is he hit 474 runs in only 14 first class innings in 1970.

Bond would have even more run-strength at his command if only Farokh Engineer would realise that to live dangerously is part and parcel of league and cup cricket but can be carried to excess in championship matches. The Indian is the soundest wicket-keeper in the country and I make no exception for Alan Knott or Bob Taylor.

His ability to 'sense' the aim of both batsmen and bowler is astonishing. In his 82 victims last summer were some dazzling examples of batsmen being caught after playing genuine leg glances. Highly spectacular as well as highly efficient Farokh is an entertainment in himself when Lancashire take the field, but he has yet to produce the runs of which he is capable. Last summer he made 797 for an average of 27.48 but with his immense ability he should be a 1,000-a-year run-maker. His eye is incredible, his footwork nimble but yet, time and time again, Engineer gets out when well set. It is all a matter of concentration. Nobody would want to eliminate the risk from the Indian's batting. It is part of the charm and the attraction of his game, yet wedded to reasonable limits it could be one

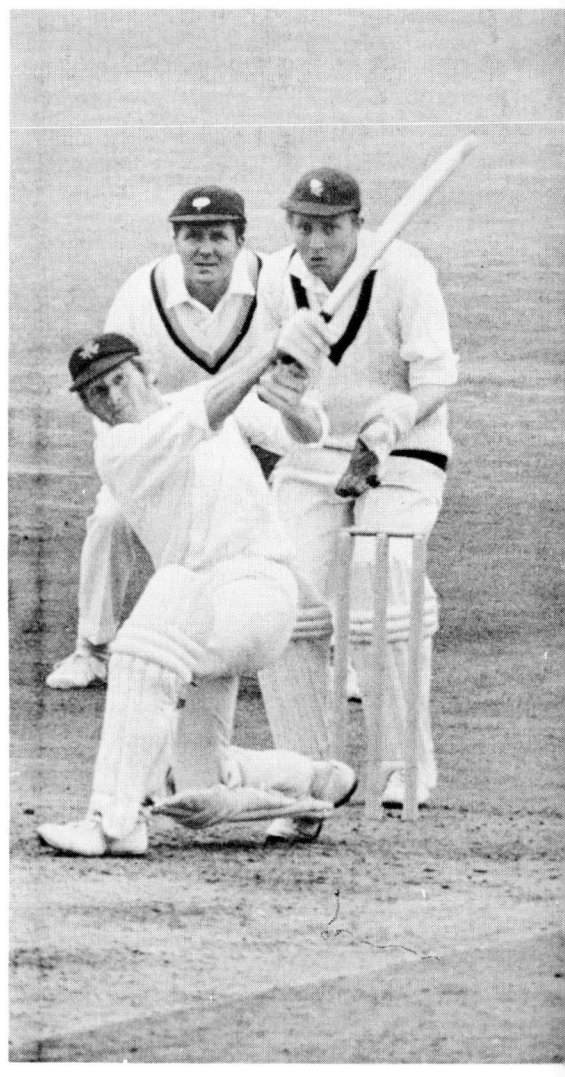

It could be the same shot by Barry Wood taken from different angles. In fact they are the shots which gave him a century in each Roses match in 1970, left at Headingley and right at Old Trafford. No wonder they look alike for both were drives for six and both were off Don Wilson.

more reason why Lancashire can become the most powerful cricketing combination of the future.

Two factors of great importance in Lancashire's rise towards the top have been the emergence of Peter Lever and Ken Shuttleworth as a pace-bowling combination. Both have been under the shadow of that great combination of Brian Statham and Ken Higgs. Now they have emerged in their own right, both gained their first Test caps against the Rest of the World, and both went with the MCC this winter.

Lever's Test appearance was not only the highlight of the season for him but also of his career to date, for he claimed a rare record by producing his best-ever figures in his international début. And what wickets he took, his haul including the best batsmen in the world. He began by having Eddie Barlow caught by Dennis Amiss and then bowled three men in a row, Graeme Pollock, Mushtaq Mohammad and Gary Sobers. Nobody could lay claim to a better trio, but the great-hearted Lever wasn't finished yet. He went on to dismiss Clive Lloyd Mike Procter and Intikhab Alam. His final figures were 32.5–9–83–7 and the crowd rose to a tired but happy bowler who had clinched his tour place in the most emphatic manner and brought England back into the game. It was not Lever's fault that he finished on the losing side . . . lightning seldom strikes twice in the same place.

Back to the county scene where Lever and Shuttleworth were often called for long and arduous spells on wickets that lacked enough pace to encourage all-out attacking. Cardiff and Edgbaston were two blackspots and at times Old Trafford produced the kind of pitch on which all bowlers were sentenced to hard labour. They never gave up and Lever took 76 wickets and his partner just two fewer.

David Hughes must wait a little longer for the representative honours that will come his way when he has learned the art of bowling on bad wickets as well as good ones. Now that seems strange for a left-hand spinner, so let me explain. On good wickets he soldiered on bravely, keeping his accuracy and taxing the batsmen with clever variations of flight and length. His spin is not vicious but can never be discounted. There were times, notably at Birmingham and Worcester, where he failed to make the most of the conditions and Lancashire were unable to clinch victory. No spin bowler is perfect at 23 but he gave us some idea of what we can expect in the future by bemusing Oxford University with 7–24, easily his best performance so far.

Howzat, yells Peter Lever—and it's the start of a memorable spell for the Lancashire paceman. Starting to walk back is Nottingham batsman Harris, lbw for 11, the first of Lever's victims in his hat-trick in May, 1969.

Hughes bowled far more overs than anyone else at Bond's command—803.3, and was the leading wicket-taker with 82. The price was almost 29 runs each wicket, all figures which suggest that last season will have taught him plenty. The most encouraging feature about Hughes is his determination to succeed and in two or three years I believe he could be another Hedley Verity.

Sharing the spinning with Hughes was Jack Simmons, uncapped, some say ungainly and unexceptional. True, on figures he had an ordinary season hitting only 423 runs for an average of 21.15 and taking 40 wickets at a cost of nearly 37 runs each. It has been said that the former Blackpool professional does not spin the ball enough, that he seldom uses his powerful bulk when batting and that at times he moves too slowly in the field.

Simmons, however, had the knack of coming off when he was most needed. They sent him in as nightwatchman at Hove and he stayed on duty throughout a good spell of the day, too, hitting his maiden century in a game in which Sussex were almost beaten. Early in the season he bowled Colin Cowdrey when Kent were hanging on grimly to avoid defeat.

Above all, throughout Lancashire's play during the season you could sense the influence of Jack Bond's captaincy. On the field he is undemonstrative but he has welded Lancashire into a strong and attractive force. His methods are simple, he has promised nothing that he could not provide. He has treated every man alike and demanded that they keep fit without imposing restrictions. Discipline has been built on good humour and common sense. Complaints have been noted and acted upon, and no man is regarded as more important than any other.

A born fighter, he could always be relied upon for runs when they were most badly needed and he sums up his own philosophy like this:

'We are all in this together. Averages mean nothing to us. Who gets the runs and wickets is not important. All that matters is that we get them and enjoy life at the same time.'

# Chapter 7

# Farokh the charming
# and disarming
## *by Brian Bearshaw*

THE first time I came into really close contact with Farokh Engineer was on a trip to Cambridge early in his first season with Lancashire. Things had not gone too well with him in his first few games and he desperately wanted to show just what he could do as a batsman. In 11 innings he was averaging only 15. 'I'm going to dig my way through tomorrow,' he declared solemnly and sincerely. When it was his turn to bat on the morrow, Lancashire were 194–2 and Harry Pilling had just hit a century. In 55 minutes Engineer, using his spade decisively, dug out 43 runs, hitting David Acfield for two sixes and one four in an over.

And that, I think, typifies this charming, disarming man. Grafting for runs is not in his soul. He is a dashing player, with an extravagance of strokes that many more 'successful' batsmen envy. He is exciting to watch, and play is never, never dull when he is around. No player can delight me more. And none can infuriate, exasperate, or madden me more. But I wouldn't want him any other way. When he stops playing his shots a light will have gone out in county cricket.

Engineer first came to the attention of the English public in 1967 when he toured this country with India, delighting the crowds with his wicket-keeping and dashing batting.

Engineer, like Rusi Surti, Nari Contractor and Polly Umrigar, is a Parsee. The Parsees, members of the Zoroastrian religious order, fled Persia after its conquest by the Arabs and settled in India in the eighth century. There are about 100,000 of them today centred around Bombay and according to the Nawab of Pataudi in his book,

*Tiger's Tale.* . . . 'Rather like the Jews in England, the Parsees are proverbial for their business ability and philanthropy. They are also very enterprising. After this tour Engineer was offered terms by Lancashire to play in English county cricket and it did not take he and his wife long to decide to take the challenge.

'I was hopeful of his success, and that he would emerge a better wicket-keeper batsman,' he concluded.

Yet his batting in that first season, 1968, was a disappointment. He played in every first-class game for the county but scored only 747 runs from 42 completed innings, figures that upset him quite a good deal. He was 30 years old in that, his first season, and it was difficult, after a life-time of playing in Indian conditions, to adapt to the slower English wickets. And he did so want to do well. His comparative failure upset him, and no matter how much consolation friends heaped upon him, he thought in his own heart that he was worthy of at least 1,000 runs in a full English season.

In 1969 he emerged more as the wicket-keeper batsman Pataudi had prophesied. He scored 952 runs in 29 completed innings to finish third in the Lancashire averages, and but for injury which caused him to miss the last four matches of the season, there is no doubt he would have reached his 1,000 runs. In this season the true character of Farokh Engineer came smiling through. He scored his first century, and also got five other 50s and showed himself a Sunday League gourmet as Lancashire strode away with this championship in its opening year.

His opening—and so far only—century for Lancashire was one of 1969's many delights. The only disappointment was that he chose to get off the ground, not at Old Trafford, where it would have been greeted rapturously, not even in England . . . but at Swansea. Batting No. 4, he scored 103 not out against Glamorgan and shared in a third-wicket stand of 121 with Harry Pilling. His 100 took him 160 minutes, and in his second 50 he hit 26 singles and only three boundaries.

He showed what a masterly batsman he could be as he played the ball almost at will to any part of the ground. He took his runs where he wanted in an impeccable way, an innings of pure pleasure.

It was in another match against Glamorgan that same season that Engineer showed his worth as a television entertainer. On a beautiful, sunny day in July Lancashire took their Sunday League match against Glamorgan to Southport. It was as well the match was televised for the ground could not hold everybody who wanted to see the game, thousands being turned away to find solace on TV.

66

Glamorgan were dismissed for 112 and in only 146 balls Lancashire romped to a nine-wicket win, Engineer leading the way with 78 not out. It was his only Sunday League 50 all season, although he averaged more than 30, but he couldn't have timed it better. He was at his exuberant best, flying up and down the wicket like a paper bag, and giving the Glamorgan bowlers and fieldsmen a terrible time. This Sunday spectacular was witnessed by hundreds of thousands of people and did the new shining image of Lancashire cricket a power of good.

Last season he had batting problems again. He scored five 50s and 800 runs and went through a bad spell or two that was sad to watch at times. Yet while his batting worries Farokh Engineer, his team-mates are genuinely unconcerned. Obviously they would like him to do even better, for his own sake, but as it was expressed to me part way through the season: 'To think he worries about his batting. The best wicket-keeper in the world and his batting bothers him. Every run he gets for us is a bonus to his keeping.'

And so it is. Only Alan Knott rivals Engineer for the title of the world's No. 1 wicket-keeper, despite the fact that he was dropped from the Rest of the World team to make way for West Indian Deryck Murray, who had not played any first-class cricket last season until he was chosen to play against England.

Engineer said little after he was thrown off the World team. True he had not batted at all well in the first two Tests, scoring 2, 0 and 1. But he took six catches and performed one stumping in the first and held two more catches in the second while he conceded a grand total of FIVE byes in England's four innings' total of 1,029 runs. And heck, when you're batting seven after Barry Richards, Eddie Barlow, Rohan Kanhai, Graeme Pollock, Clive Lloyd and Gary Sobers, you can be forgiven a batting failure.

But although he said little, Engineer was obviously hurt. He has a good deal of pride and it was wounded, but it wasn't long before he was his old ebullient self again, relaxed and utterly at ease.

And while the Rest of the World discarded him, Lancashire skipper Jack Bond was never stinting in his praise of his wicket-keeping. 'People think Clive has lifted this team,' he once told me. 'There's no question Clive has done wonders for us. He's given us confidence and taken a good deal of the pressure off. But Farokh started Lancashire on the way back in 1968 and a lot of the praise about our fielding today is due to the example this man set. He was so lively in the field, he made poor returns look good and lifted everybody's game.'

Farokh Engineer shows his power
and style with a legside four.

Charge! Engineer does his famous
dashing-down-the-wicket shot.

Engineer is a natural athlete with a wonderful eye that is as evident in his work behind the stumps as in front of them. He likes plenty of room when he keeps wicket, and many of his catches are taken in front of first slip, leaping with lightning reflexes, and rarely, so rarely, letting the ball go. He is the height of elegance and England has not often seen such a graceful, competent wicket-keeper. He is never anything other than friendly and on his way to change ends between overs will frequently stop for a word with the batsman.

But while his wicket-keeping touches the peak of style, his batting can occasionally touch the depths of despair. An innings against Glamorgan at Blackpool last season was typical. It was obvious from the start that nothing was going right. His timing was awry, he looked like a novice and no matter what he did the bat simply refused to strike the ball in the proper manner. His hopelessness was clear to everybody and he was soon rushing up and down the wicket, swinging his bat like a scythe.

Malcolm Nash was the bowler from the Stanley Park end when Farokh made one typical swipe that was intended to dispatch the ball first plop into the boating lake. But no such luck. He had advanced a good six yards down the wicket to make sure of contact and in face of this ferocious charge Roger Davis, fielding at silly mid-on—damn silly as it turned out—covered his head with his hands and fell to his knees, whether in horror or prayer I never discovered. Engineer was almost alongside the unfortunate Davis when he made contact and with Nash deciding on a full follow through, there was a right little gathering in the centre of the pitch as the ball took off vertically like a rocket from a launching pad.

It was a most comic situation. Engineer, his bat still whirling, Nash trying to sight the ball yet avoid falling over Davis who was still kneeling, as yet oblivious of the scene unfolding around him. Suddenly the actors froze, just for a moment, while the ball, its power spent, hurtled for home by the same path it had just taken.

Engineer was rooted, but Nash quickly came out of his trance and bellowed at the other member of the triumvirate to get up off his knees and get into the action. Or words to that effect. Davis looked up, Nash on his one hand, Engineer on the other. The ball plummeted down just over an arm's length away. Nash couldn't move for it because of the various obstructions around him, so Davis shuffled towards the ball on his knees and thrust out his arms, like a poor beggar hoping for a crumb.

He managed to get a touch, but the ball fell to the ground. Nash, hands on hips, looked down at the prone figure of Davis, while

Engineer beat a hasty, gleeful retreat to the safety of his crease. 'He'll get a hundred,' I thought. In fact he got four in 45 minutes before another almighty heave sent the ball skywards yet again. Calm and method prevailed this time, however, and the wicket-keeper took the simplest of skied catches.

There cannot be a batsman in the game, and this includes the West Indies, Wales, Canada or Fiji if you like, who likes to leave his crease and charge the bowlers the way Engineer does. It's as if the wickets have turned into cobras. In a Sunday League game against Kent at Blackheath, David Lloyd watched from his crease as Engineer raced down the wicket to a ball from John Dye. 'I thought he were coming for a chat,' said Lloyd.

But it was Glamorgan's Ossie Wheatley who summed it up perfectly in the Sunday game at Southport in 1969 when he said to Bond: 'I don't mind him charging me, but would he let me set off first. . . .'

It's all good for the crowd, but it can be shattering for his team-mates. Anybody batting with Engineer in this mood has to be fast and firm on his call for a run. And if he can make his decision while the bowler is still on his way to his mark so much the better.

But whatever his faults, I have the greatest admiration for Engineer, a difficult man to ruffle, and typically Indian in his desire to please. He will talk to anybody—and for a long time, too, on any topic, and is the most considerate of men with children. If he is practising before the start of a game he will draw youngsters in by hitting the ball in their direction. He encourages boys to bowl and field to him and one of the most pleasant sights at an English ground is to see the youngsters running from the ends of the ground just to be near this world-class player.

'When I was young, it disappointed me when some of our great players would have nothing to do with me. I like children and if there's anything I can do to encourage them I will.'

His efforts were noticed at Blackpool one year and in a nearby evening paper a few days later there was a letter from a man praising Engineer. 'While there's this sort of man about,' he wrote, 'cricket has nothing to fear.'

As might be expected, he is an affable companion when the day's play is ended. He is thoughtful and generous and I well remember going to a new Indian restaurant with him in London's Lancaster Gate one Sunday evening. We were to have Tandoori chicken, but unfortunately the chef was ill and the cooking was being done by the manager, while the one waiter was an inexperienced young

The infuriating Farokh . . . bowled
playing across the line.

Jumping to it is Farokh Engineer
as he takes a high return.

On behalf of the Manchester and Salford Students' Rag committee, Farokh Engineer hands over a cheque for £1,771 15s. 1d. to Mrs. W. E. Payne for the Royal Manchester Children's hospital.

Englishman, dressed in flowing robes and a turban. The service, not unexpectedly, was poor, but the climax came when Farokh asked the waiter for a finger bowl. The waiter looked perplexed and headed off for an assistant manager who had been hiding at the pay desk.

The assistant manager came. 'A finger bowl, sir, to wash your hands,' he said. 'Please,' said Farokh. The assistant manager went to the waiter and hurriedly whispered something in his ear. The waiter went downstairs. 'He must think I want a drink,' said Farokh. It was nearly five minutes later before the waiter re-appeared, bearing a small plate made up of different coloured glass. He carried the plate delicately, resting it on the tips of his upturned fingers and thumb. Proudly he set it down, the plate bearing a hot, wet flannel soaked in eau de cologne. The waiter said nothing, but his face told all. 'Finger bowl?' it said. 'Not in a high-class establishment like this.' Farokh also said nothing. His face, too, was a picture.

New contracts to Lancashire's players means Engineer will be with us at least until 1973. His wicket-keeping again will be enough to guarantee him his place, but I fervently hope he can reach his 1,000 runs for the season.

I hope, too, that there will be at least one century at Manchester to add to those he has scored in Swansea, Calcutta, Hyderabad, Bombay, Madras and Perth. But whatever he does, I shall still get

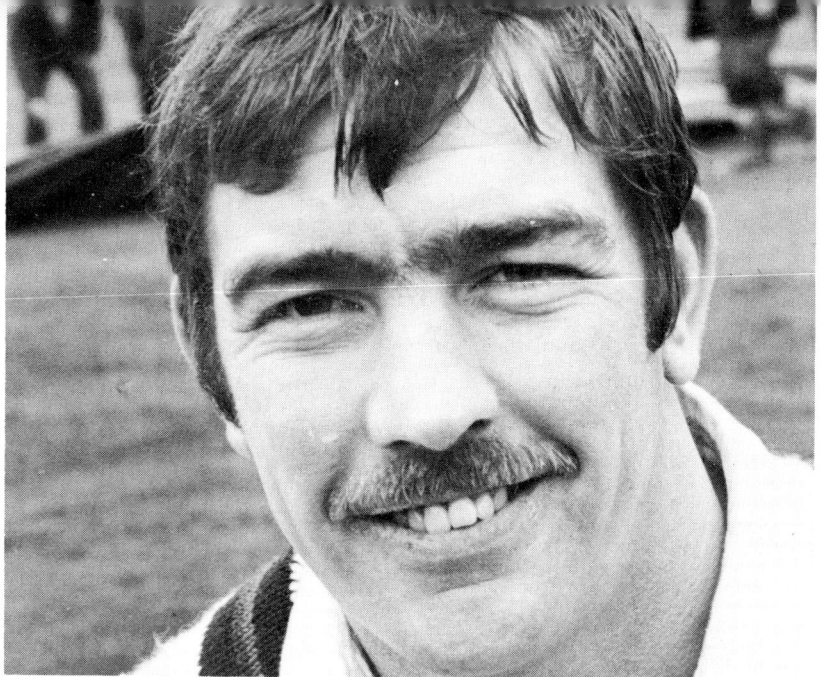

Keith Goodwin who was outstanding as deputy wicket-keeper to Farokh Engineer.

the greatest delight, the utmost pleasure, in watching him play and enjoy cricket.

However, before leaving the wicket-keeping business I must comment on how lucky are Lancashire to have such a fine deputy for Engineer in Keith Goodwin although the two couldn't be bigger contrasts. Engineer has the flamboyance of the East while Goodwin is a solid Lancastrian.

When Lancashire played Hampshire at Southampton last season one experienced observer described Keith as among the best half-dozen stumpers in the country. That might have been an over-statement, but it is indisputable that Goodwin would not have any difficulty in holding his place in several other counties.

Yet, although he has been a regular first-teamer in only three of his eleven years—between the sacking of Geoff Clayton and signing of Engineer—he doesn't want to leave.

'It would mean leaving everything,' he said. 'I could, perhaps, get in a team somewhere else and still not get paid as well as with Lancashire. Then there is a benefit coming up.'

Goodwin, too, has been doing one of the most important jobs in the club, captaining the second team where he must groom the next generation.

# Chapter 8

# The long and short of it
*by Eric Todd*
(*The Guardian*)

LANCASHIRE'S resurgence-renaissance might be nearer the truth—
last summer was hailed with a satisfaction and pleasure which
extended far beyond the bounds of Old Trafford. Yorkshire's chairman Brian Sellers told me that he was really delighted that the
'old enemy' had returned, albeit belatedly perhaps, to their rightful
place in the limelight, and this I considered to be among the highest
of the compliments and tributes which poured into Old Trafford.

There were, of course, isolated instances of cynicism and envy
('They'll never keep it up'), and one or two people were quick to
point out that it was coming to something if a county couldn't win
something without imported assistance. Where, they demanded,
would Lancashire have been without Farokh Engineer, an Indian,
Clive Lloyd, a West Indian, and Barry Wood, a Yorkshireman?
And Harry Pilling surely was a native of Lilliput rather than one of
Ashton-under-Lyne? Even in triumph, Lancashire had their
critics.

Not that it worried them one little bit. They had proved themselves to be the team of the season, and they had fulfilled their
avowed intent to entertain the public. And if they had wished to be
cynical in their own turn—which they did not—they could have
pointed out that with the inevitable exception of Yorkshire, none
of the counties was home grown so to say. All had strangers within
their gates. The only difference was that Lancashire had made
better use of theirs, and if they had carried off the championship title
and thus completed a unique hat trick, it would have been no more
than their initiative and brilliant cricket had deserved.

74

The long and short of it batting together. Harry Pilling hits out against Somerset with Clive Lloyd watching at the other end.

Results and statistics told their own tale although Lancashire's triumphs were not to be assessed in terms of figures alone. The remarkable team spirit, the happy atmosphere on and off the field, the captaincy of Jack Bond, and the capacity or determination of any player to make good the temporary failure of a colleague transformed Lancashire into a combination of awesome strength and of even more formidable potential because if any man be unwise enough to suggest that Lancashire's success last summer were a transitory thing, then he had better think again. Given better fortune than they have had in some of my 23 years' close association with them, Lancashire will be in the forefront for many years to come.

In view of all the circumstances, it might seem at once invidious and unfair to make individual appraisal of the summer of 1970. Indeed, with some counties it might well be fatal so temperamental and 'touchy' are a few of the illustrious. I well remember one occasion many years ago when I criticised a well-known player for his slovenly fielding. He waylaid me later in the day and remarked 'You don't criticise me. Don't forget I'm an England player'. Which is by the way although it just goes to show.

Collectively and individually, Lancashire won more plaudits last summer than some teams earn in a lifetime so that I don't suppose for one minute that the rest of the players will feel slighted if I write my piece about Harry Pilling and Clive Lloyd. After all I was invited to do so and not necessarily because they were or are better than anybody else. The long and the short of it is. . . . And I'll take the short first.

To the best of my knowledge, Pilling first appeared on the Old Trafford scene in 1959 when he finished 17th in the second eleven batting averages, and 14th in those of the club and ground side. For the latter, however, he took third place in the bowling averages behind Peter Marner and Colin Hilton. In fact only Freddie Moore took more wickets than Pilling who returned better figures then such stalwarts as Malcolm Hilton, Roy Tattersall, Ken Howard, and Tommy Greenhough. One of these days I must ask him why he gave up trying to be an all rounder!

By the beginning of last summer, Pilling had collected 6,543 runs and nine centuries in first-class cricket for Lancashire, and still the best of him was yet to come in spite of a send off which would have convinced a lesser man that this was to be the year of the locusts. He scored 66 and 2 against Kent at Dartford, then Leicestershire dismissed him for 10 and 0, Oxford University for 2, Northamptonshire for 12 and 5, Yorkshire for 9, and Kent, in a vengeful mood for 9 and 28 at Old Trafford—143 in ten completed innings. He asked for and was given a game with the second eleven, but self confidence avoided him there as well and he made no more than 37 for once out against Northamptonshire second eleven at Old Trafford.

June nevertheless bust out all over for Harry Pilling, and he took 507 runs off Gloucestershire, Warwickshire, Essex, Hampshire, and Nottinghamshire. He scored 109 and 69 against Gloucestershire at Old Trafford, and in the next game there he made a century not out in each innings against Warwickshire. This particular 'double' had been performed already for Lancashire by J. T. Tyldes-

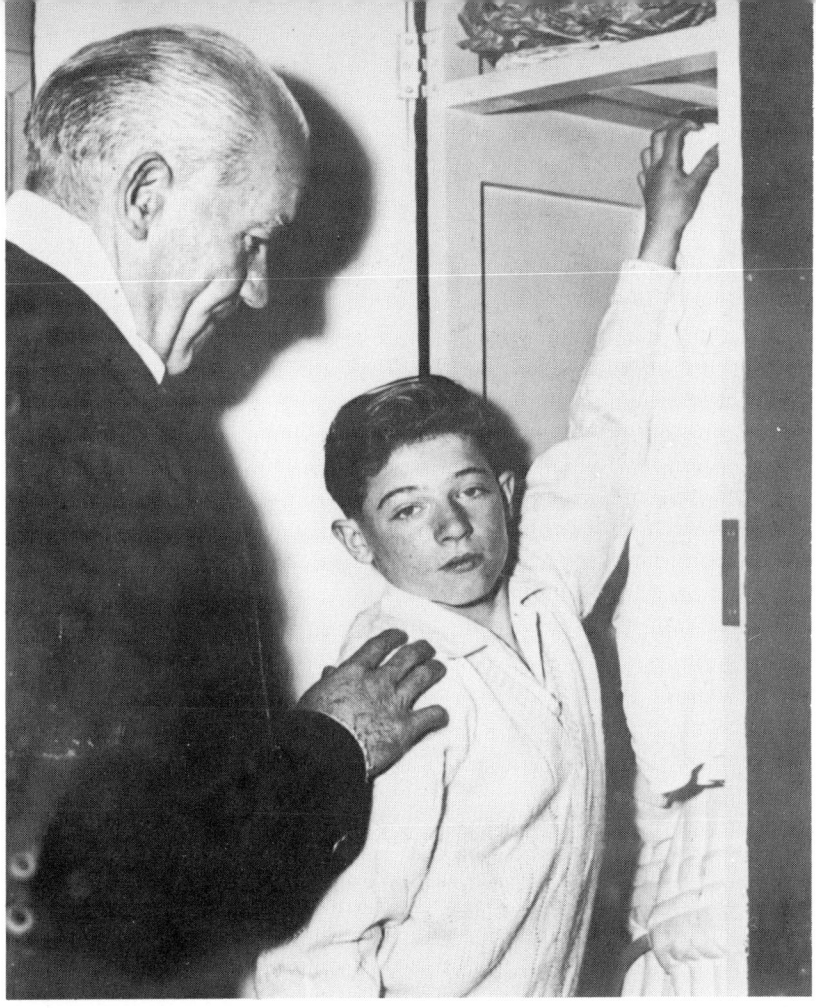

Recognise this little fella? It's Harry Pilling being introduced to Old Trafford by then coach Stan Worthington when he first joined the county in 1959. And Harry has difficulty reaching the top of his locker!

ley, Charlie Hallows and Eddie Paynter (all against Warwickshire incidentally), Winston Place, Ernest Tyldesley and Cyril Washbrook. The two Tyldesleys and Hallows in fact scored two centuries in the same match on two occasions, although among this select group, Hallows alone had carried his bat twice—against Leicestershire at Ashby-de-la-Zouch in 1924.

A week after Pilling had thus added his name to the record book, he made 120 not out against Middlesex at Old Trafford. Many people—and not all of them in the North by any means—decided that Pilling was a certainty for Australia this winter. He didn't quite make it, but it was a near thing.

In the event Pilling calmed down after June and appeared to concentrate on winning the Gillette Cup and the John Player League. From July to the end of the season, he experienced comparative drought in the county championship although he had two useful innings of 40 and 63 at Hove where he silenced those spectators who had waxed sarcastic at Lancashire's earlier slow batting. He made 66 in the first innings against Yorkshire at Old Trafford, and finally produced an excellent 89 at Cardiff where he spent 40 minutes nursing a single. The stocktaking revealed that Pilling had cleared 1,000 runs for the fifth time in six seasons.

Apart from his exploits in the county championship, Pilling adjusted himself readily to the more urgent requirements of the John Player League and the Gillette Cup tournaments. In the former, he failed only once to reach double figures—ironically enough against Gloucestershire whom he had punished so severely the day before—and his considerable aggregate of 615, which included five scores of 50 or more, enabled him to become the first batsman to compile 1,000 runs in this competition. On two occasions he appeared as a No. 6 bowler and he dismissed Barrett of Leicestershire and Denman of Sussex for three runs. When invited to comment on his success as a bowler, Pilling replied 'Ah just foxed 'em'.

In the Gillette Cup, Pilling contributed modestly to the victories against Gloucestershire and Somerset, and he was bowled by Hampshire's White for nothing at Old Trafford. But in the final Pilling, dropped at cover by Ken Suttle when only 16, went on and played a decisive part in the overthrow of Sussex. He and Engineer added 72 for the fifth wicket, and in victory these two not were divided. Pilling rightly was chosen by Alec Bedser as man of the match, and this probably was the highlight of the season for this remarkable little man of whom it was said eleven years ago that he was far too small ever to make the grade in first-class cricket.

The game has known batsmen more proficient technically and more prolific than Pilling, but there have been few more popular, few who by sheer application and personality have won so many friends among spectators and opponents alike all over the country. Women in particular looked upon him with a kind of maternal, protective interest considering it a shame perhaps that such a little man should be asked, nay ordered to stand up to nasty fast bowlers especially when they played with a hard ball.

But nobody need ever worry about Pilling. He can take care of himself although I wonder sometimes why he doesn't use the hook stroke more often as an additional gesture of defiance. As it is, he has one of the best cover drives in the business born of strong arms, keen eyes, and a massive heart. He is also a very fine fielder especially in the outfield where he acknowledges the applause of the crowd with a cheeky grin and maybe an aside which, alas, cannot be overheard in the remoteness of the Press box. Certainly he would have held his own against the famous Hill at Sydney. Well, it's not too late yet.

Pilling has a well developed sense of humour which if less Rabelaisian then Colin Hilton's, nevertheless has caused some consternation —but never reprehension—in high places. He can and often does clear the stuffy atmosphere and I enjoyed particularly the story they tell about one visit to a 'posh' dinner in London. Harry found himself sitting next to a titled, bejewelled lady, and at the end of the meal by which time her ladyship had been reduced to a state of nervous exhaustion, Harry asked if he could take the identification card from her plate. 'Ah'd like missus to see what sort o' company ah keep when ah'm away from 'ome,' quoth he.

A character and a man of character.

Long before he exploded on the Lancashire scene, Clive Lloyd had stamped his personality and authority on the game the world over. Everywhere he went, people paid just to see him walk on to the field. If he scored runs, so much the better. If he did not, well he was usually good for a few wickets. If he were bowled for nothing and took no wickets for plenty, no matter. He could still field. And everywhere he went, the plaintive cry could be heard 'I wish we had him'. The gods, in collaboration with enterprising officials, sent Lloyd to Old Trafford.

He made a quite inconspicuous first appearance for Lancashire in 1968, and he arrived belatedly in the 1969 season making ten appearances in first class matches. He scored 554 runs finishing at the top of the batting averages with 39.57 having ended the term with 88 and 99 against the New Zealanders at Old Trafford. Cricket in general and Lancashire in particular waited impatiently for the passing of winter's long shadow.

Lloyd's start last summer was conventional and probing, two modest contributions of 28 and 14 against Leicestershire, but between 9 May and 10 June, he amassed 767 runs in eleven innings, once not out. He hammered 163 off the Kent bowlers at Dartford, 121 at Oxford, 102 against Gloucestershire at Old Trafford, and against Warwickshire, also at Old Trafford he graciously allowed Pilling to take the giant's share of the plunder while reserving the right to make 58 and 73 for himself. Against Essex at Ilford, Lloyd

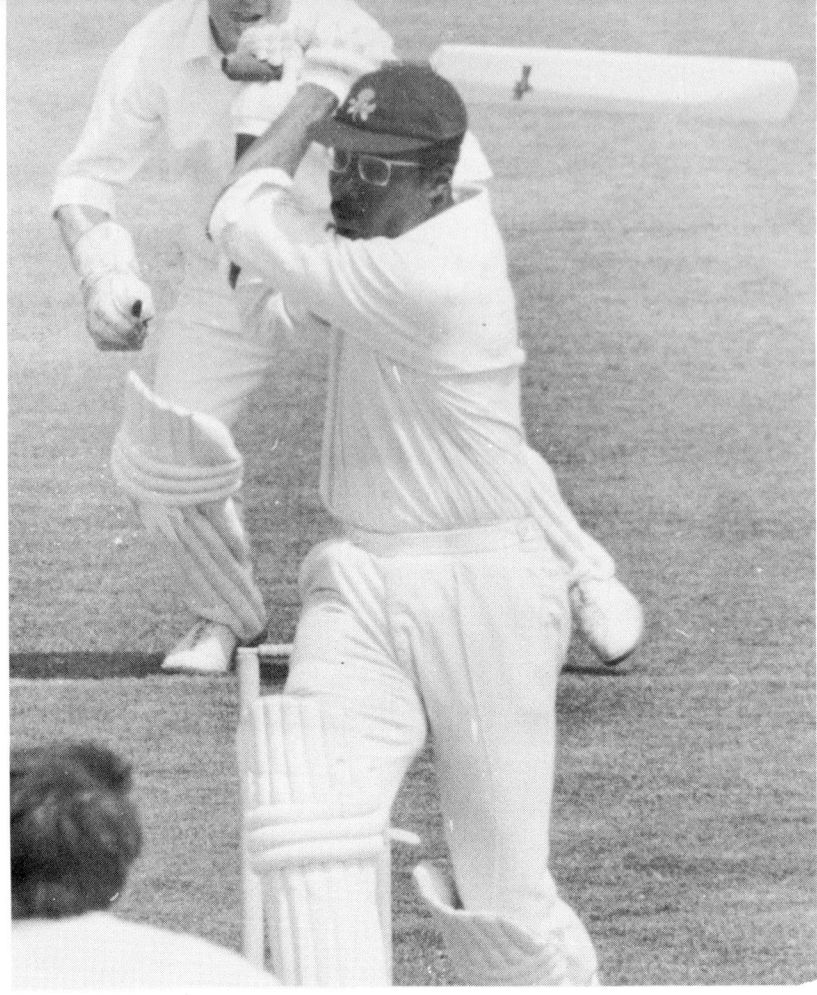

A bowler's eye view of a big hit by Clive Lloyd.

made 19 in the first innings and one at the second attempt as Lancashire made a brave but unavailing attempt to beat the rain and
Essex. Thereafter until late in August Lancashire were deprived of
his regular attendance because of Test calls although he was available
for John Player League and Gillette Cup games. He ended the
championship season with several useful knocks including three half
centuries.

Not having seen all of them, I am not qualified to suggest which
was the best of Lloyd's many fine innings but in Kent at least they
still talk with awe of his contribution at Dartford—163 in 173
minutes off 121 deliveries. He hit seven 6s—with one of which he
reached his century—and 18 4s, and property repairers and insur-

ance brokers look forward eagerly to his next visit. From Dartford, he went to The Parks and completed a century in 95 minutes off 84 deliveries and when at last he was caught by Carroll off Bryant, he had hit six 6s and 11 4s. His 102 against Gloucestershire included two 6s and 14 4s.

Lloyd turned the John Player League into a glorious carnival although it was not until early June that he made a score of character-istic dimensions—90 against the hapless Gloucestershire attack at Old Trafford. He hit two 6s and nine 4s before he was caught brilliantly by Brown off his own bowling. Later that afternoon, Phillips made a magnificent 116 not out off 113 deliveries for the visitors, and for once in a while even Lloyd looked slightly envious.

The second Sunday in July found Lloyd in his most violent mood as he smote 134 off 74 deliveries against Somerset at Old Trafford with four 6s and 15 4s. Thereafter, he inclined towards mercy, but at Cardiff on 9 August he again harnessed himself to a whirlwind and in 52 deliveries, he hit 63 with five 6s and three 4s. A record crowd for the ground of 7,000 was reduced to near hysteria. In 14 Sunday innings, four of them not out, Lloyd collected 423 runs. And at Dudley, where he failed with the bat, he took three wickets for 22 and dismissed Worcestershire's Headley and Turner with catches which one spectator described as 'inhuman'. Sunday was no day of rest for bowlers and fielders when Clive Lloyd was in the neighbourhood. Like Jehu, son of Nimshi in quite different circum-stances, Lloyd drove furiously.

In the Gillette Cup, Lloyd made 157 in four innings, his highest score being at Bristol, 53 in 50 minutes. In the final at Lord's, he contented himself with 29 but still left the spectators drooling over one superb on drive for six. Lloyd seldom disappointed anyone, least of all himself.

Roget would have been pushed hard to have found an adjective fitting enough to describe Lloyd's fielding. Lloyd certainly proved himself worthy of a place among the greatest cover points in history, and some of his catches—notably those at Dudley and that at Aig-burth where he dismissed Mushtaq of Northamptonshire with a catch which Mushtaq will remember for the rest of his days—defied adequate description. His reflexes were uncanny and his returns to the wicket-keeper were models of accuracy. His aim could not be faulted and if Engineer happened to be placed unfavourably—which was not very often—then Lloyd was capable of hitting the stumps from any angle and from any distance. Nobody in his right mind even considered the possibility of a quick single if the ball

A man with an unusual job in the winter is Harry Pilling—he is a
salesman for a firm of undertakers. And here he studies the merchandise.

were hit in the direction of Lloyd. Only if Lloyd were not playing
were risks taken by an opposing batsman.

I enjoyed comparing Lloyd with that other fine Lancashire
fieldsman, Alan Wharton. Wharton would gallop after the ball using
his arms like railway engine pistons to generate more speed, and
having overtaken the ball, he would descend upon it in the manner
of a vulture. Lloyd never galloped. He prowled stealthily but swiftly
and then swooped on the ball rather than pounced on it.

The most amiable among men, Lloyd sometimes conceals the
galvanism which is the most telling weapon in his formidable
armoury. I have seen him go to the wicket with his bat trailing
rather like a woman towing a shopping basket on wheels to the
supermarket. I have seen him strolling about the field in between
overs his eyes directed aloft as if seeking contact with the cricketing

"Oh" Harry Pilling seems to be saying—the actual words were probably stronger—as he turns to see a stump uprooted then playing against the Indian touring team at Southport in 1967. The obviously delighted bowler is Guha.

gods who have endowed him so generously. At times he has appeared 'miles away' as they say. Until the ball has been hit to within 30 yards of him. Then. . . .

Off the field, Lloyd is a man of simple tastes although he has a mild passion for music of any description, the louder the better. One of these days I have no doubt he will go in to bat with a transistor radio in his pocket. He also enjoys driving a car—provided it be fitted with a radio. On one occasion, he gave a lift to a colleague on

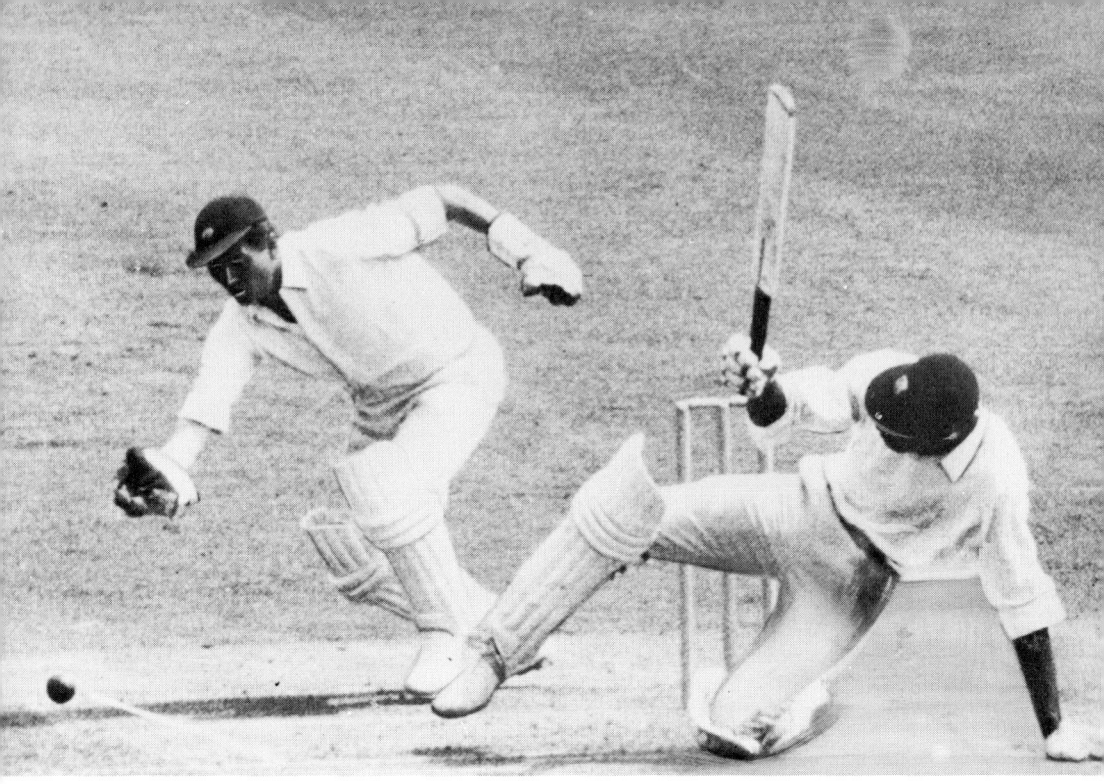

Clive Lloyd has not only all the shots in the book but a few that defy description as well which is perfectly shown in this picture as he drops to his knee to play a one-handed shot.

a journey to London. Inevitably the radio was working overtime. On the M1, Lloyd put his foot down on the accelerator and his passenger began to look somewhat apprehensive as the speedometer needle reached a figure more in keeping with an average innings by Lloyd.

'What's the matter?' asked Lloyd solicitously 'Is the music disturbing you?'

It is fitting perhaps that the epilogue to this particular chapter should concern Harry Pilling and Clive Lloyd as partners. A sight to end all sights, surely. The highlight of their association undoubtedly was their 231 against Kent at Dartford, but only slightly less memorable were their 179 in 133 minutes against Gloucestershire at Old Trafford, and their 90 in 12 overs at Cardiff. In the John Player League, they put on 182 in 80 minutes against Somerset, and a brisk 88 against Northamptonshire at Aigburth. They simply could not be kept out of the news—except in June when during a brief strike in the newspaper industry they took Warwickshire apart at Old Trafford with stands of 95 and 131 (in 85 minutes).

Pilling, for all his enthusiasm and skill was hard put on occasions to keep up with his ebullient partner who threatened to lap him in the glorious chase for runs. So too did Engineer. At the end of the Sunday match against Somerset, I went in search of Pilling and found him quenching his thirst and recovering his breath in a remote part of the pavilion.

'What' I asked him, 'is it really like to bat with Clive?' Harry reflected for a moment and then replied with feeling 'It's a' reet. But ah were a bit freetened ah'd got trodden on'.

Characters. And men of great character.

*Chapter 9*

# The Kop comes to cricket
*by Vernon Addison*

IN SPORT they also serve who stand and don't even watch. For devotion to the cause there was the cloth-capped man, whose station was behind a stand at Oldham's Rugby League ground. It was in their palmy days when full-back Bernard Ganley—incidentally also a useful Central Lancashire League cricketer with Crompton—made the art of goal-kicking look merely a simple geometric exercise and his shots at one end invariably cleared not only the bar but the stand, too.

Each goal to Bernard was just another job done but as the ball was sailing over, another job was just starting behind the stand. While Ganley received the crowd's appreciation his cloth-capped colleague was going unacknowledged but just as happily about his business, unshakeable in the belief that he, too, had a vital role to play. His job? To ensure that the ball was not borne off by the inevitable gang of boys to be found there and to return it promptly to the field of play. Quite a busy job it was too in those days.

In the army of unsung sports heroes he joins the legion of gatemen who rarely see a match but without whom no game would be played. A good gateman can be an artist in his own right, informing latecomers of the score, his intelligence being gained purely by the crowd's noise. The supreme artists can not only tell you that United are a goal up but that they missed a 'sitter' and their goalkeeper had saved a penalty!

Life is not quite the same, however, for the poor cricket gateman for who can work out whether it's a wicket or a boundary by a mild ripple of half-hearted clapping? At least it wasn't the same until

86

This Daily Express picture perfectly illustrates how the Kop has come to cricket. They are mostly youngsters—and note the handclapping—who are celebrating Lancashire's second John Player League title after the final match with Yorkshire.

87

Lancashire started revitalising the game. This I discovered last season when I found some plausible reason for slipping out of the office early one afternoon to head for the Gillette Cup-tie with Hampshire. As the bus pulled up in Chester Road a thunderous noise made us wonder whether to turn right for soccer's Old Trafford or left for cricket's Old Trafford.

But left it was and another roar followed at the entrance to the ground where a delighted gateman announced, with full confidence in his information: 'That's another one out . . . Hants will be five for about 83'.

By the end of the season I'll bet that gateman could not only tell you the score but how many sixes Clive Lloyd had hit!

For the most important point of 1970 may yet turn out to be not so much that Lancashire did the one-day double of the John Player League and Gillette Cup; not so much that entertainment came back to the game; but that this was the year that the Kop came to cricket, the time when the youngsters rediscovered the game and flocked to support it. This could be the brightest omen yet for the future of the game. These newcomers brought with them the enthusiasm and brashness of youth and their soccer-style chants of 'Lan-ca-shire' . . . 'Pilling for England' (alas, ignored on high) . . . 'We are the champions' . . . would shame the famous Sydney Hillites into silence.

Oddly enough this Lancashire cricket choir gave its first full performance on an away game and owed much to skipper Jack Bond losing the toss. The match was against Derbyshire on 20 July and as it was at Buxton so many thought it ideal for a day out that it is generally accepted that only about 2,000 of the 8,000 crowd were from Derbyshire.

With the weather threatening, both captains, Bond and Ian Buxton, had decided that, given the chance, they would put the opposition in. The opportunity fell to Buxton and within nine overs he didn't appreciate it for openers Farokh Engineer and Ken Snellgrove had plundered the incredible total of 77 runs. Such is the spirit of Lancashire that Farokh spurned personal glory, recklessly running himself out in sight of the fastest half-century, having made 46 off only 26 balls. Snellgrove, unperturbed about not holding a regular place, hit 30 and then followed 40 by Harry Pilling, 22 by Clive Lloyd, 20 from John Sullivan and a fine 53 by the newest member of the side, Frank Hayes, as they piled up 229–9 in 39 overs.

A polite round of applause would have been an affront to this brand of exciting entertainment . . . and that's how the Kop came

Down—but not out—is Ken Snellgrove, who with Farokh Engineer made such a blistering start to the match against Derbyshire, the day Lancashire's Kop choir was born.

to cricket. The *Daily Express* was quick to appreciate the new phenomena and the next day, besides a full report of the match, which Lancs won by 114 runs, James Lawton captured the scene like this:

'If they ever arrive at Lord's—as they promised to in tempting thousands at Buxton cricket ground last night—they will look and sound as out-of-place as washboards in the Halle.

'But cricket's newest phenomena—Lancashire's young coach-borne followers who chant and roar with Soccer-style abandon—are unlikely to be embarrassed.

'These lads, whose fathers were brought up on League cricket, have discovered the joys of one-day cricket, as a young man might savour his first taste of good whisky.

'And if their manner of satisfaction should offend the Establishment, well, that is no concern of theirs.

'The cricketers of Derbyshire certainly felt the raw force of this support as they crumbled before the Sunday League's runaway leaders.

'Across the serenity of the Buxton setting, a timeless set piece for cricket, there came a continuous wave of chants . . . "Harry Pilling for England" . . . "We are the champions" . . . and, most emphatically: "We'll be running round Lord's with the cup".

Every Lancashire success, however minor or fleeting, was greeted with rapturous cheers . . . every Derby slip, however trivial, was the cause for their harshest censure.

'It was a strange background to the usually sedate matter of winning or losing a cricket match. But its enthusiasm was infectious, and is clearly the most encouraging development of this season, when the national game fights for its life.

'Certainly there were few complaints in the Buxton "box office", where they were still counting the proceeds a good hour after the end of play.'

From then on no home match was complete without the Old Trafford glee club. Their members even travelled in numbers to Dudley, where it is estimated that just under half of the 7,000 crowd was from Lancashire.

Coupled with their pulling power Wilf Wooller, chairman and former skipper of Glamorgan, dubbed Lancs the 'Manchester United of cricket'.

But what made the youngsters turn to the game that has so often been described sneeringly as providing entertainment for the retired and the clergy? Jack Wood, the Lancashire secretary, believes there are two reasons: 'First, youngsters of today love to be associated with success whether it be sport or the pop world. Then, the team spirit has communicated itself to the public'.

Wood maintains that 'the happiest place in England, possibly the world, is the Lancashire dressing room these days. They say there are no characters now but don't you believe it. Five minutes in the Lancs dressing room and you will agree with me that they are all great characters', he says.

'If John Sullivan is 12th man he really wants Frank Hayes to get a century because it's not for Hayes but for Lancashire. It's the

Jack Wood, the down-to-earth Lancashire secretary who came to cricket from Rugby League.

All part of the day's work for a secretary. Jack Wood sees to the signing of David Bailey during the 1967–68 close season. Bailey, who previously played for Durham in the Minor Counties, is a brilliant fielder and forcing bat, averaging 41.33 in the second team in 1970. Yet he was unable to get one game in the senior side—more proof of the depth of Lancashire's talent.

same with all the players who have had to stand down.'

Two stories involving the secretary and the skipper to illustrate the wonderful and infectious spirit of the team.

The first was when Bond, before leaving for an away game, called at the office of Wood who suggested that it was going to be a really tough match. 'Yes,' replied Bond, 'but whatever happens we'll enjoy ourselves.'

The second was between innings in that Sunday match with Worcestershire at Dudley. Lancashire's total of 168 did not look nearly enough and when Wood voiced his fears Bond replied in a manner of which Churchill would have been proud: 'It simply means that we have to bowl better and field better than we have ever done.'

They did just that and won by 37 runs.

There is nothing patronising or inhibiting in Lancashire's attitude to their new fans and when an old member complained that he thought these young fellas were a bit much Wood tartly replied: 'We have spent years trying to get them here and when they come you complain. We are delighted to see them and delighted with their behaviour.'

Such complaints were isolated but that member might yet have a few more liverish turns for Wood, with the true mind of a secretary, sees these youngsters not merely as new supporters but as possible members.

'Everyone who pays his six bob to watch Lancashire is a potential member to me,' he says, 'Nothing would delight me more than to see some of these young lads—yes, with banners and all, call at my office to join.'

Such a refreshingly down-to-earth attitude isn't too surprising to those who know Jack Wood, for he was brought up in the hard world of Rugby League, where you have to count your blessings like the takings, carefully for neither are ever over plentiful. Before coming to Old Trafford he had been secretary of Huddersfield and Wigan, two RL clubs which had known good times and bad.

Nor is he worried about hooligan behaviour that has marred soccer. 'There must have been about 30,000 inside Old Trafford for that final Sunday League game with Yorkshire and they were all wonderfully well behaved,' he recalled.

'Many of them had never been to a cricket match before, but environment does help and the newcomers soon got the hang of what to do—and more important, what not to do—from the more experienced supporters'.

'They can scream, chant and shout to their heart's content and even run on the pitch at the end. All we ask is that they don't stop the game such as running on to congratulate a century-maker'.

# Chapter *10*

# The young brigade
*by Vernon Addison*

THE greatest pleasure in being nothing more than an average club cricketer is to have played against youngsters who are destined for stardom. In this respect I can claim a notable hat-trick having faced Frank Hayes, David Hughes and Gerry Knox before they were even a gleam in a Lancashire scout's eye.

Such talent-spotting can be a salutary affair, however, as I found against Hayes when he was playing for Marple. He can barely have been 16 years of age and fewer in runs when I dropped him down the legside behind the wicket. Next delivery—and it wasn't all that far off being good length—he moved into position so quickly that he had time to give the ball a look of disdain before hooking it not only over the square leg boundary but clearing, too, an oak huge enough to have hidden most of Robin Hood's merry men. Frank then went on to hit 70-odd in about 12 overs.

Hughes was younger—about 14—when he, too, topped 70 for Newton-le-Willows . . . and he didn't need any assistance from me. While no one pretends that our standard of play was high these were tremendous performances against fully-grown men, some of whom had had their moments of glory.

Knox, too, was about 14 when I played against him in our native Northumberland where he, like the other two, displayed a mature range of shots for one so young. Even then these boys were a class apart.

So it was with particular interest that I watched Hayes explode on to the first class cricket scene last season where he was greeted with all the fervour of a 'white hope' in heavyweight boxing. For opening

Duck! And it's another four to Frank Hayes with a powerful legside shot.

the floodgates to the top world stars was only the first step in resuscitating county cricket—to complete the cure the game needed to prove that it could attract and produce top-class home-grown talent. The advent of Hayes was viewed as being as important in the long term as the importation of Clive Lloyd.

The Hayes story had started long before I muffed that one-handed catch. Like Colin Cowdrey it began with a cricket-mad father, Frank Senior, himself a more than useful club performer and knowing him, too, I am sure that had his surname started with a 'C' young Frank could have found himself with the initials L.C.C. It takes, however, more than initials to make a cricketer and Frank Senior took the first positive steps when he laid a concrete pitch in his back garden, covered it with matting and bought a net. From then on they spent every spare moment at practice.

Young Frank was such a natural that before he was 10 he was playing for Marple in the High Peak Junior League against boys up to the age of 17. Nor was his progress hindered by running out his father when they opened the innings. It was Dad's call, but young Frank sent him back and they ended in the position we club cricketer's know so well—within hand-shaking distance in midwicket. 'It should have been me who went but Dad, who had made only six, walked off,' recalled Frank, who went on to make 41.

The next year—at 14—Frank was in the Marple first team in the Lancashire and Cheshire League, a competition of high standard.

Milestones were now slipping past as quickly as driving along a motorway. He won the High Peak Junior League batting averages with the incredible figure of 97.2 and in the next few years topped both the Marple and Lancashire and Cheshire League batting.

At 17 he met up with Lancashire—and Jack Bond for the first time —playing against them. For he made his début for Cheshire against a strong Lancashire second team which included Jack Bond, Ken Higgs and Bob Bennett and some promising youngsters called David Hughes, David Lloyd and Ken Shuttleworth. It was Bond, too, who caught Hayes off Higgs but not before he made an excellent 37.

His first taste of top-class cricketers left him amazed at the pace off the pitch of the apparently medium-paced Higgs. 'That day he was much faster than Shuttleworth,' said Frank.

Unfortunately Frank Hayes senior was now dead, but his influence remained. He had been an object lesson to the fathers of all sports-gifted boys. He kept both his own feet and those of the eldest of his four sons firmly on the ground, instilling into the boy that before

96

*Left:* A close-up of David Lloyd at practice.
*Right:* David Hughes who had the most successful season of his career in 1970, being Lancashire's leading wicket taker in the county championship with 82 victims. He was fourth in the national averages for the John Player Sunday League.

ever contemplating a cricketing career he must make sure of his future by going to university. Dutifully young Frank went to Sheffield University where he collected a second class honours degree in physics and mathematics and further honours at sport, playing for the 'Varsity at Rugby and soccer as well as cricket and turning out for the U.A.U. at the last two. In the U.A.U. soccer side he played alongside Steve Heighway, who burst on to the soccer scene last season with Liverpool as explosively as Hayes did with Lancs.

During the vacations Frank, who was born in Preston in December 1946, played for Lancashire seconds and as soon as he qualified it was taken for granted that he would join the staff. In fact he felt like packing the game in altogether.

'I had gone stale and was cheesed off with the game,' he said, and if you are surprised that a young man in his twenties can be browned off with a game that offers so much, you must realise that already he had played more cricket than many good players do in a lifetime. 'I had been playing almost seven days a week from about the age of 15 or 16 without a holiday, unless, that is, you call a cricket tour a holiday.'

Even more amazing for a player who was to take the second half of the 1970 season by storm, he doubted his own ability!

'I had played four seasons for Lancashire seconds and never scored a century,' he explained. 'I saw players like Gerry Knox, David Lloyd and Mike Beddow get "tons" in the second team and yet fail in the firsts. I thought if they can't make it what chance is there for me?'

Bowlers who suffered at his hands last season will be equally amazed to hear that at this time he had trouble with his eyes and had taken to wearing glasses. This was probably brought on by studying and has since cleared up.

Eventually he was persuaded to sign for Lancashire but even so he was full of self doubts. 'I couldn't see how I could possibly get in the first team and the best I hoped for was to get my second eleven cap inside two years.'

Perhaps here it is worth digressing and thinking for a moment what part luck plays in sport. For instance, in retrospect, Lancashire profited by failing to sign Gary Sobers. While Sobers is undeniably the world's greatest all-rounder he has been unable to inspire Nottingham as Clive Lloyd has done at Lancashire, possibly because Lloyd has his future in front of him while Sobers has done just about everything possible in the game.

The cancellation of the South African tour to England last year had a silver lining of good fortune for Lancashire—and Hayes. The county officials knowing that they would lose Clive Lloyd and Farokh Engineer, thought little of the substitution of a Rest of the World series—yet these Tests were to emphasise the depth of Lancashire's talent and hasten Hayes' entry.

For it was in place of Lloyd that Hayes made his début against Middlesex at Old Trafford—and his future as a fieldsman may well have been moulded by a chance incident. He was normally an out-fielder but on the previous day he 'threw' his elbow in practice and so was put in the slips. This has long been a problem position for Lancashire and when Hayes marked his first day's play with two catches his fielding future had been decided.

Spectators consider the slips the next best thing to a rest home, but Hayes' memory of his first day was of being very, very tired. 'All you do in the slips is bend, concentrate and get up . . . but it's darned hard work,' confessed Frank.

98

If he slept peacefully that night then he is one of those lucky people who could doze off on a clothes line, for the last 20 minutes of the day's play was enough to enduce nightmares in the most experienced of batsmen. Middlesex had declared and let loose John Price—on his day as fast as they come—on a baked, lightning-fast track. He removed David Lloyd and when he bowled night-watchman Keith Goodwin the watching Hayes swore that the batsman didn't have time to even move his bat before his 'furniture was flying'.

'His pace was awe-inspiring', Frank summed up succinctly.

The morrow brought further disaster and Hayes strode in for his maiden innings at a confidence-shattering 47–4, to be followed by Ken Snellgrove, who has never been certain of a first team place in his career at Old Trafford, at 57–5.

What can a captain say to a young batsman going out for his first innings in such a difficult position? Rather like writing letters of condolence, no words ever seem adequate. But Bond, with yet another demonstration of his gifts of leadership, found the right touch when he said: 'Remember, Frank, you've played against really first class cricketers many times before in the second team. This is no different.'

Frank, however, was to find in his first over from Price that things were different. But first he faced Keith Jones, and Hayes had a slice of good fortune that we wish on all newcomers—a full toss third ball. Now a full toss is the same whether bowled in the High Peak Junior League or the county championships. Although Frank has always been rated a nervous starter even in his league days he showed no signs of it as he gave that ball its just deserts . . . four.

Then came Price and Frank takes up the commentary himself. 'I have always been able to hook and when he dropped one a little short I thought this was my chance. But I hadn't even got into position for the shot when the ball hit my shoulder. I had never known anything so fast.'

Hayes, however, and Snellgrove too, weathered the storm. But there was another lesson—if not so painful—for Frank when Middlesex turned to the spin of Fred Titmus. Again there was something new for him in the swinging slow bowler. 'I had never seen a slow man move the ball in the air so much as Titmus. Time and again I was preparing to sweep a ball that seemed going well wide down the legside only to have to hurriedly change my shot and play defensively off the stumps.'

Yet outwardly the Lancashire pair seemed imperturbable and

how refreshingly they went for their shots instead of trying to dig their way out of trouble. Hayes even hit two sixes. The applause that greeted their half-centuries would have done credit to a crowd many times the size of the moderate midweek gathering.

In the newspaper offices of Manchester—and we trust London, too—they were preparing the inevitable headlines, 'Hayes' dream début', as he went into what are generally known as the nervous nineties. To Frank, however, it was more a case of having come through the exhausting eighties for in his own words he was 'dead tired'. And this fatigue almost certainly cost him the supreme start to his cricketing career, a century.

At 94 he tried to hit Peter Parfitt over the top but for once he failed to get hold of the ball properly and was caught by Keith Jones at mid on.

The missing six runs didn't make any difference to the members' appreciation. The total was now 248, Hayes, who had also stroked a high quota of 15 fours, and Snellgrove having put on 191. Those few who were there were already cherishing the thought that for years to come they would be able to tell the story of seeing the birth of a Lancashire star. They gave him a standing ovation and as Frank raised his bat in appreciation he felt well pleased with his performance.

But by the time he had reached the dressing room the awful truth had dawned on him. 'What a stupid fool I have been,' he thought 'I have thrown away the chance of a lifetime for no-one remembers your nineties.'

In his case I would doubt it for after getting an equally promising 45 in the second innings he was to fall one short of a century in just as dramatic circumstances.

With two overs to go and two wickets left Lancashire wanted 27 runs to beat Hampshire at Southampton. You might say that they don't write situations like that in schoolboy fiction any more. Maybe, but the spirit of Lancashire had already been so imbued into Hayes that there were no thoughts of making sure of his hundred or stitching up for a draw—the target was victory.

With Bob Cottam operating at the other end Frank calculated that if they were to pull it off they would have to score the bulk of the runs off slow left-handers of Peter Sainsbury.

Sainsbury, as befits any self-respecting member of long standing in the spin bowlers club, is also well versed in the art of mind reading, at least batsmen's minds. So, his first ball of the second last over of the match, was thrown invitingly a little higher. Alas for Hayes, a shade wider, too, and for once Peter gave it a tweak. Frank accepted the bait, went for the big hit only to miss the ball and be easily stumped by Bob Stephenson.

The entire Hants team led the applause all the way back to the pavilion and afterwards Sainsbury said: 'This was an unusual wicket for me as I usually get my stumpings "through the gate", but as I bowled I noticed Frank coming down the wicket.

'He certainly is a most promising player. I've not seen him play a defensive innings but he impressed me as an attacking player not afraid of going down the wicket and giving the ball a whack. He's got all the shots and could well play for England if he keeps improving.'

Hayes, who is much better at long innings than long speeches, merely said: 'Sainsbury kidded me all right. But missing my century didn't bother me this time for we were going for victory for the team.' His 99 took only 130 minutes and included one six and 18 fours . . . 78 runs in boundaries.

Hayes never did get that century but he played plenty more good innings to end his first season with an impressive average of 37.84, totalling 719 runs from 22 innings, three of them not out.

He scored 75 against Somerset at Southport and yet said, with a natural humility, of Tom Cartwright, the wily former England medium-pace bowler: 'Mr. Cartwright—(note the "Mr.")—troubled me all the time. I have never seen the ball move like it and lost count of the number of times I played and missed.'

Hayes marked his first Roses match with 82 not out and then said he owed it to Clive Lloyd. 'I had reached about 20 when I thought I should begin to slog out. Clive saw this and told me to play for myself. That doesn't at first sound like playing for the team but, when you think about it, you are not playing for the side if you get yourself out stupidly. I wouldn't have got anywhere near even a half century but for Clive.'

Ever ready to hand the praise elsewhere he feels that he owes much, too, to such experienced players in the second team as John Savage and Graham Atkinson, who, towards the end of last cricket season, became secretary of Salford Rugby League club. 'I was always going for my shots too early and getting out in my teens. They kept impressing on me that I had to take more time playing myself in.'

There's still a schoolboy look about Frank Hayes and his modesty is unaffected by demands for his inclusion as a learner batsman in the M.C.C. party that went to Australia and New Zealand this winter, a campaign that was started by no less a figure than former Lancashire skipper Ken Grieves, in his weekly article in the *Manchester Evening News*.

Frank remains shy and quiet, too. They proudly sat him in the seat of honour at the Lancashire and Cheshire League dinner in October when his club, Marple, received the trophy for the sixth time on the run, this time sharing it with Longsight. Yet he was happy to travel to and from the dinner with his Marple club-mates in a mini-bus and the quietest man on the journey was Hayes.

If the tour selectors did not accept Grieves' gratuitous advice they acknowledged Frank's potential by selecting him for the under-25 team against an England XI at Scarborough and he proved his worth with half a century.

Hayes arrival on to the scene has, understandably, tended to overshadow other members of Lancashire's up-and-coming brigade. Who, for instance, can recall Ken Snellgrove's exact score in Hayes' first match against Middlesex? The answer is 138 and yet Ken had to play second fiddle in the publicity.

Snellgrove is in his late twenties, could walk into most other county teams and has time still to earn a regular place at Old Trafford, although the competition could not be fiercer.

Two men who have time on their side, are David Lloyd and David Hughes, and many good judges believe that like Hayes they, too, could eventually play for England.

Skipper Jack Bond was bitterly disappointed that Lloyd did not join Hayes in that Under-25 team, believing that there were players of lesser ability than David in that side. Hampshire certainly seem to appreciate the full potential of Lancashire's youngsters for in his book last year their captain, Roy Marshall, named Lloyd as one of the three most promising cricketers in the country.

Lloyd has a thankless task, for being an opening bat at Lancashire these days is rather like being the first turn on a variety show. A polite round of applause, a little action and then it's get off to make way for the big stars. At least that's how the public tend to see it but, of course, the longer the openers stay the more likely are the big hitters, Clive Lloyd, Farokh Engineer and Johnny Sullivan, to do their stuff.

Lancashire have just the pair in Barry Wood and David Lloyd to lay a solid foundation from which the entertainers can perform in style. Lloyd has tended to be overshadowed by Wood, too, who had his best season but topped 1,000 runs for the second season running despite missing three weeks with a back injury.

A trio who prove that Lancashire's future is safe . . . *left*, Frank Hayes, *bottom left*, David Hughes, and *bottom right*, David Lloyd.

He has subjugated his natural style for the team's sake and those spectators who have yelled 'get on with it' would be surprised at the full range of shots he displays in the nets.

Opening bats like good wines get better with age and like good lovers improve with maturity so Lloyd's age is further tribute to his ability. He was born in Accrington in March 1947, which makes him decidedly on the young side for this vital role. Many think of him as being older for he has been at Old Trafford since 1965, making his début that year and gaining his cap in 1968.

He is also the latest in Lancashire's list of converts from bowling to batting. In recent years there was Brian Booth, who came as a leg-spinner and No. 11 bat and worked his way up to being an opening batsman who once came close to scoring 1,000 runs by the end of May before being allowed, some think surprisingly, to join Leicester. Then it's hard to believe that Harry Pilling was first considered a back-of-the-hand spinner while Lloyd was first hailed as a left-hand spinner. He took 27 wickets in 1966 at a cost of 23.85 each, but since then his batting has taken such prioroty that in 1968 he bowled only 20 overs.

David Hughes, too, is a left-hand spinner and while he is also worthy of a higher place in the batting order there is no danger of his switching allegiance for last season was his most productive being the side's leading wicket taker. Lancashire's growing faith in him is shown in the increased overs he has been asked to bowl, as well as the steady increase in wickets over the past three years.

| Overs | Maidens | Runs | Wickets | Average |
|---|---|---|---|---|
| 1968 | | | | |
| 265.1 | 95 | 644 | 29 | 22.20 |
| 1969 | | | | |
| 445.3 | 171 | 1,116 | 44 | 25.36 |
| 1970 | | | | |
| 803.3 | 248 | 2,377 | 82 | 28.98 |

Hughes was also born in 1947—in the month of May in Newton-le-Willows—joined the county in 1966 and won his county cap last season.

It has been suggested that he rolls rather than spins the ball, but it is not a theory subscribed to by either the Lancashire team nor Oxford University.

Hughes had his career best figures of 7–24 against the University last year and Bond says: 'He can spin it all right when the wicket is helpful. More important, though, he is very accurate.'

Hughes has also developed a lethal swinging yorker as he showed in the Gillette Cup final, when it claimed the wickets of the dangerous Jim Parks and Tony Greig at a vital time.

It must be disheartening to opposing sides to see Hughes come in as low as No. 10 and display classical drives. 'He's very good off the front foot and deserves to be going in higher. In many teams he would be five or six,' says Bond, adding with a chuckle, 'but what can you do when the skipper can't get above No. 7?'

If Hughes needs any incentive to stick at his batting he should remember that the last Lancashire player to do the double was also a left-hand spinner, Len Hopwood, who did the feat in 1934 and 1935.

Hayes . . . Hughes . . . and Lloyd . . . the Lancashire future seems safe enough in their hands, a trio who have come up together through the Lancashire schools and Lancashire Federation teams. A trio, who, says Bond, make him feel old. 'Look what they have achieved already—and I didn't come on the staff until I was 23.'

# Chapter 11

# Pride returns to Lancashire
*by Brian Bearshaw*

*Before the success seasons of 1969 and 1970 Lancashire had 15 England players in the post war era. The impressive list is: Bob Barber, Bob Berry, Ken Cranston, Tommy Greenhough, Ken Higgs, Malcolm Hilton, Nigel Howard, John Ikin, Winston Place, Dick Pollard, Geoff Pullar, Brian Statham, Roy Tattersall, Cyril Washbrook and Alan Wharton. In only three seasons in this period, 1949, 1962 and 1967 did they fail to have a bowler taking 100 wickets, often they had two and in 1959 and 1960 they had three, Statham, Higgs and Greenhough. Yet all they could manage was joint champions once—in 1950—and only occasionally, and certainly not recently, did they promise more. In the past two home seasons the only England caps were one each by Ken Shuttleworth and Peter Lever against the Rest of the World last season. No one took 100 wickets yet Lancashire are at last a force in modern cricket. True their successes have been in the one-day game and they have world-class performances in Clive Lloyd's batting and Farokh Engineer's wicket-keeping. Taking Test caps as the criterion, however, the present side is not as star-studded as many since the war and yet by general consent this is the best team in the truest meaning of the word. In this chapter BRIAN BEARSHAW talks to past and present players to discover the reasons behind the transformation.*

JACK BOND sat on one of the comfortable benches that run round the visitors' dressing-room at Lord's. He was clad only in his cricket shirt and socks, one leg crossed underneath him. The start of the second day's play against Middlesex was 45 minutes away, and most of the Lancashire players were at the nets.

In this match last season Lancashire were already in a commanding position, well on the way to their 10-wicket win. They were flying high in the championship table, top of the Sunday League and six days away from the Gillette Cup semi-final match against Somerset at Taunton.

Bond looked round the famous dressing-room. It is a vast place, pictures from the past look sternly down from the walls, and if you close your eyes in the quiet of the day you can imagine Grace and Hammond, Bradman and Lindwall, Hutton and all sitting right there alongside you.

'I think of the players that have been in this room,' Bond mused. 'I think of the famous, the outstanding Lancashire players I've been with in here. Some great players, yet together what did we achieve? Then I think of these lads and what they've done by playing for one another.'

Some weeks later I was at Lord's again for an informal Press conference with Mr. David Clark, manager of the M.C.C. tour of Australia. When the discussions were over I went upstairs, along the now darkened corridor and back into the dressing-room. I took a closer look and studied the pictures on the wall, even the one of the Fijian team that toured New Zealand in 1895! And there was one of dear Cec Pepper, a thinner Cec Pepper with the Australian Services team that played here just after the Second World War.

There were enough hooks on the walls for four cricket teams and one wall was lined with lockers. On a table was laid a huge clock, its fingers pointing to 11.32. My mind went back to that morning with Bond, when he spoke with almost fatherly affection about his team. I recalled looking around at those left in the dressing-room. Farokh Engineer had been buckling on his pads, almost ready for a net. Here was a world-class wicket-keeper with strong claims to being THE best.

There was Harry Pilling, recalling the days when he and another wicket-keeper, Geoff Clayton, dressed only in jock straps, used to tone up with a spell of wrestling, Mossley style, before each day's play. Clive Lloyd was away playing against England, but Ken Shuttleworth, with one Test match behind him, and Peter Lever, still to be chosen by England, were looking at the day's newspapers. The others were at practice. Barry Wood, Ken Snellgrove, Johnny Sullivan, Frank Hayes, David Hughes, Jack Simmons.

These men, with the addition principally of the injured David Lloyd, had taken Lancashire back into prominence, restored the county's pride, made the crowds swell again at Old Trafford. When

A significant picture. Ken Higgs reads out the telegram which tells him that he has been elected for the 1965-66 tour of Australia. Third from left is David Larter, the Northants fast bowler who also went on the tour and on this day was playing against Lancs. The other players are, left to right, Harry Pilling, Geoff Pullar, Tommy Greenhough and David Green. Only Pilling is still at Old Trafford and the others have all tasted ups and downs. Pullar and Green joined Gloucester while Higgs and Greenhough went into league cricket.

the season was over with Lancashire Gillette Cup and John Player League winners and third in the championship table, their highest position for 10 years, I asked Harry Pilling what he thought had brought about the change. He talked of team spirit, of every man playing for the team, nobody thinking only of himself, of a settled team which brought confidence to every player, of people's faith.

'Not so long ago you played each game so you'd be chosen for the next,' he said. 'You had one or two bad innings and you were out. Now you can have a bad run and you're helped through it. When other people have confidence in you, you have confidence in yourself and your whole game improves.'

108

In his own way Tommy Greenhough, who played with Lancashire from 1950 until he was sacked at the end of the 1966 season, said very much the same. But his finger pointed more directly at the heart of the reason for Lancashire's failures through the greater part of the 1960s.

'There was too much interference on team selection from committeemen,' he declared. 'Too many noses were stuck in and too often we went on the field knowing it wasn't our strongest team.' Greenhough himself suffered from this interference and in the 16 years he played first-class cricket for Lancashire this England leg-spinner had only two years uninterrupted cricket with the first team. At times he was dropped in favour of vastly inferior players. Experienced cricketers in other counties watched with astonishment—and often with relief when they were playing against Lancashire—when players of the calibre of Greenhough, Peter Marner, Roy Collins, Geoff Clayton, Jack Bond, Ken Higgs and others were dropped from the team.

*Left:* Tommy Greenhough was a leg spinner and googly bowler fit to play for England yet suffered tremendously through interference at Old Trafford.
*Right:* A big hit from Roy Collins but his potential was never fully developed in Lancashire's in-and-out days.

There was a saying among the players at Old Trafford whenever they lost in those days: 'Famous heads will roll.' Invariably they did. There was hardly a player who knew with any certainty whether he would be in the team for the next match. Talk to almost any player about an approaching visit to say the Oval or Hove and you couldn't say many words before the phrase 'If selected' was thrown in.

Players naturally became selfish. This was their living. The next game was important to them and their families and it wasn't surprising if some began to play for themselves.

The batsman who was good enough could avoid the bowlers he disliked and hog the ones he fancied. If a particular bowler bothered him he was good enough to take a single at the start of the over to get a rest period in the bowler's crease. Once there he wouldn't be moved, except to run safe two's. If, however, he faced a bowler who was giving no trouble at all, he indulged himself in only twos and fours. It needed an equally wily man at the other end to force him to run singles and threes, unless it was the end of the over, of course.

Greenhough even recalled occasions when runs were wanted quickly, but batsmen refused to go for them until they had been at the wicket some time, until they had enough runs to satisfy them their position was secure.

'It's a bit harder for a bowler to play for himself,' he said. 'But if he is established he can decline to bowl for various reasons, or if he feels like it, suggest he goes on to bowl. Look at the times Ken Higgs was dropped. But we knew his value, always bowling uphill or into the wind. Peter Lever had it rough for a long time. He rarely had the new ball, he could bowl well, take none for 40, but he wouldn't be brought back for a go at the last three or four.'

These were unhappy days at Old Trafford. Players and committee-men drew far apart, many players lived in dread of the season ending, wondering whether they would be retained or whether they would be out of work. And for many, this happened season after season.

In Greenhough's benefit year of 1964 the season dragged well into August and still players had not been told of the club's plans for the following season. Players, annoyed and frustrated at the delay, were at Clitheroe for a benefit match for Greenhough, whose wife aired her displeasure at the position. Midway through the afternoon a member of the benefit committee went to her. 'You've no need to worry,' he said. 'Tommy's all right.' Members of the benefit committee knew, players didn't.

There was far too much officiousness and highhandedness in the

*Left:* Geoff Edrich—one of the famous cricketing family and, according to Roy Collins, the "best man Lancashire never appointed."
*Right:* Peter Marner fixes photographs in his Saddleworth home. Marner was one of the players sacked by Lancashire and later joined Leicestershire. He retired at the end of last season and has signed a two-year contract with Todmorden in the Lancashire league.

club. Interference was regular and Greenhough thought it ran from the time Cyril Washbrook finished being captain in 1959 to some time during Brian Statham's reign.

Greenhough held Washbrook in high regard. 'When he said something he meant it,' he said. In those days players who were offered re-engagement terms were given a slip of paper to sign, declaring their acceptance or rejection of terms. Greenhough knew other counties were interested in him and he wanted the chance to establish and prove himself. He declined Lancashire's offer in 1958 and returned the slip to the secretary's office. 'Within 15 minutes I was called to see the captain,' he said. 'I explained the position to Washbrook who told me that wickets would be covered the following season and that I would be in his team at the start. "Then it's up to you," he added.

Greenhough decided to re-sign and in that 1959 season took 120 wickets and played his first game for England. The following year he again took 120 wickets, the only two full seasons Lancashire had faith in their talented leg-spinner and googly bowler.

Roy Collins also attributed Lancashire's decline to bad management. 'It stemmed from the top,' he said. 'And there were too many appointments of poor captains. You know, the best man Lancashire never appointed was Geoff Edrich. Here was a man, very much like Jack Bond who knew how to get the best out of each player, who was ready to talk to anybody. He knew the ones to encourage and the ones who needed the whip.'

Jack Bond said in an interview last season that there were times at Old Trafford when he thought they were prepared to pick anybody but him for the team. They were despairing days, but they have gone. Lancashire's team is now the strongest available, and it is settled.

Four men played in every championship game last season—Bond, Wood, Pilling, Hughes. Jack Simmons played 23 of the 24 games. David Lloyd missed the four in July through injury, while four more —Clive Lloyd, Engineer, Lever and Shuttleworth—would have played every game but for international calls or injury. Johnny Sullivan played in 19 of the matches and the usual panel of 13 was made up by Frank Hayes and Ken Snellgrove.

And there wasn't an ounce of selfishness from all the players put together. David Hughes ran off a string of three 'ducks' midway through the season, but when Bond needed quick runs, Hughes put his own considerations to one side and played his strokes in the team cause. He scored only seven, but there was no complaint from Hughes, but plenty of praise from Bond.

# Lancashire's Post-War County Championship
## Record & Captains

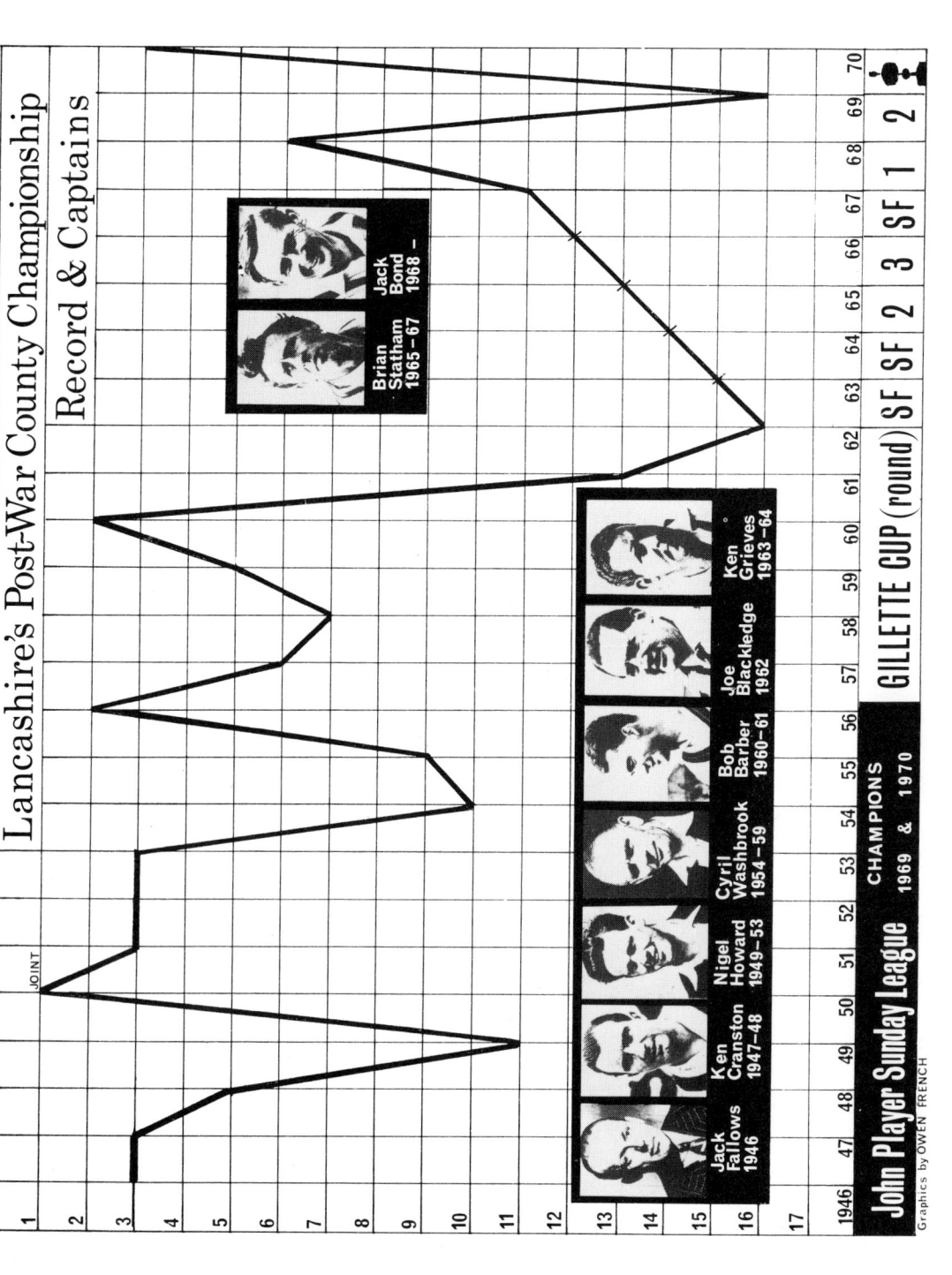

Jack Fallows 1946
Ken Cranston 1947–48
Nigel Howard 1949–53
Cyril Washbrook 1954–59
Bob Barber 1960–61
Joe Blackledge 1962
Ken Grieves 1963–64
Brian Statham 1965–67
Jack Bond 1968 –

John Player Sunday League CHAMPIONS 1969 & 1970

GILLETTE CUP (round)

| | 63 | 64 | 65 | 66 | 67 | 68 | 69 | 70 |
|---|---|---|---|---|---|---|---|---|
| | SF | SF | 2 | 3 | SF | 1 | 2 | |

Graphics by OWEN FRENCH

# Chapter 12

# Down among the 'dobbers'
## by Vernon Addison

CRICKET isn't only the game played by the likes of Lancashire where the shots come out of the book and the whites from the latest detergent test.

There is also the game where grass-stains on trousers are forms of battle-medals, ties are for keeping up the pants, where turn-ups are tucked into the socks when the outfield is long and damp (as often it is) and the shots, if they come from a book, then it is more often the agricultural guide.

This is the cricket of the poet, where the vicar opens the batting with the blacksmith . . . although the only time that I ever played with a clergyman he batted more like a blacksmith.

He had only two aims in life—to put us all on the path of righteousness and all bowlers over the mid-wicket boundary.

In one particular innings which reached the seventies he heaved the opposing team's star bowler into the next-door meadow half a dozen times—all from good length balls on the off-stump. After the last one the exasperated bowler could stand it no more and stormed down the wicket to blaspheme:

'Christ, "vic", you haven't played a Christian shot all afternoon.'

That's village cricket for you.

Whether they have any reverends playing I don't know but it's the cricket you can find not so far from Old Trafford in the hill country around its borders of Derbyshire, Cheshire and Lancashire. There's a rustic ring about the names . . . Haughton Dale, High Lane, Hawk Green, Buxworth Hope Congos, Trinity Methodists, although, perhaps, some of the places are not so delightful as their names sound.

My first introduction into the High Peak League in which these clubs have all at one time played came, inevitably for me, after seeing to the Saturday sports edition. Arriving at the game just after tea I was greeted by a charming young lady who said: 'We're having a smashing match—we've had two dobbings already.'

To those of you who have suddenly discovered that you don't know all the terminology of cricket, let me explain that dobbing is the art of running up to bowl but instead running out the non-striking batsman without the courtesy of a warning.

To my club, High Lane, falls the doubtful distinction of having the king of dobbers, Jack Cliffe, an artist at his work showing a great sense of occasion and drama when he performs the deed.

Take a cup-tie last season. Jack nodded an acknowledgement as the opposing captain came in to bat—and then dobbed him before he had faced a ball. Even this however is not his piece de resistance. This was a few years ago in a league match at Mirrless when High Lane were going for the title. Feelings ran high from the outset for, after rain delayed the start, High Lane felt that the opposition, who had nothing to gain, were dragging their feet in getting the game started. High Lane even pitched the stumps themselves but no sooner had the umpires positioned the bails than they were off. Jack pulled off his master stroke . . . a dobbing with the first ball of the match.

Recently he was re-telling the story for the umpteenth time in our unofficial headquarters, The Bulls Head, when one of our new members, Keith Leigh, asked Jack if he knew who the unfortunate batsman was.

'No,' said Jack, 'I can't remember.'

'Well, I can. It was me,' said Keith.

Jack was quite unembarrassed by the appearance of this ghost of dobbings past. For his logic is: 'I wouldn't do it if it wasn't legal.'

Jack, however, disclaims credit for the supreme dobbing of them all. This happened in the days of National Service when an enthusiast from Buxworth flew home at his own expense on a 48-hour pass from Germany just to play. His reward? To be dobbed without facing a ball.

Our Mr. Cliffe can be the perfect gentleman and he laughs about the time he did hand out a warning. They were playing Parkside and as it was their first season in the league Jack thought they might not yet have got the hang of things. So when he found one of their batsmen setting off to run before he had reached the wicket he stopped and warned him of the consequences of such rashness.

'Thanks,' replied the batsman. 'You won't catch me like that again.'

But Jack did . . . the very next ball. 'I had to laugh,' said Cliffe—but not before he had removed the bails.

Perhaps by now you have a mental picture of Dobber Jack. It might then surprise you to learn that he is a successful businessman who runs a Jaguar and thinks of his holidays in terms of a cruise.

Don't get me wrong either, I have more time for Jack than most on a cricket field. I have played with him and against him when we have crossed words and swords. What I like about him is that there is none of your 'let's-make-a-game-of-it-and-give-everyone-a-bowl' nonsense. Even on a Sunday friendly he believes in getting the opposition 'done' as quickly as possible. So do I.

For those of you who believe that dobbing isn't quite cricket—as the saying goes—I refer you back to chapter one. The famous Barlow was a forerunner of our Jack. Come to think of it, why should you warn a batsman who is flagrantly cheating? For the batsman deliberately beating the gun is almost impossible to run out.

I have never tried dobbing myself—simply because I have been asked to bowl only once in the past 20 years and that against the staff of one of my son's schools. There are limits to all things. If you fancy becoming a Barlow or Jack Cliffe I should warn you that it is as well to check first with U Thant to see if he has a few troops to spare from policing the trouble spots of the world. For after a dobbing you need a peace-keeping mission between the teams, I can tell you.

Cricket has always been a game for characters, but the first class game with names like Freddie Trueman, Johnny Wardle, Sid Barnes, David Green, umpire Cec Pepper and co. doesn't have them all to itself.

In Buxworth they can match those names with a whole family, the Hills.

Jack is the father and although sons Bernard and Alan are good enough to have had spells with Derbyshire he rules them with patriarchal discipline, both on and off the field. It is rumoured that one of the boys thought that he could improve his game by joining a bigger club in another league but dad sharply told him where his place in this sporting life was—with the village club.

Dad also has his own ideas about his role when batting with his boys . . . as caller-in-chief and coach.

So when Jack and Bernard put on a big stand against High Lane one day the at-the-wicket dialogue went on interminably like this:

'One run, lad'.

'Right, Dad'.

'Hit them beggars, lad'.

'Yes, Dad'.

'Two runs, lad',

'O.K., Dad'.

'Leave them alone, lad'.

'Right-o, Dad'.

Youth, however, can never be totally suppressed and when the stand was in sight of the century mark Bernard plucked up courage.

'One run, Dad', he called.

'Nay, lad', came the reply.

Bernard, realising the rank folly of his impetuosity, pulled on all brakes with the inevitable result. He ended flat on his back in the middle of the wicket and by the time he got up it was to see a grinning bowler deciding which bail to ever so gently remove.

Returning to the pavilion Bernard called:

'Dad'.

'Yes, lad'.

'You're a right twit'.

Or something like that.

Buxworth, the opponents swear, has a weather all of its own. When you can see the hills, the saying goes, it is going to rain and when you can't—it is. Nevertheless they boast of a proud record for getting matches played whenever everyone else is rained off.

Marple, however, who are now resplendent as champions of the Lancashire and Cheshire League for six years in succession (the most recent shared with Longsight) remember their more modest days and an occasion when Buxworth weren't so enthusiastic to get the game on. It was near the end of the season, Marple were going for the High Peak title and Buxworth had nothing at stake.

It had rained but as soon as the hills became visible Marple wanted to get started.

'Never play before next season', was the Buxworth verdict.

'All we want is some sawdust', replied Marple.

'Haven't got any'.

But the championship wasn't going to be lost for the want of a bag of sawdust. 'Surely there was some in the village?'

'Oh, yes,' and a man's house was named.

'How do we get there?'

Then followed a most intricate list of directions, which would have done credit to the whole map department of the A.A. When, finally, the speaker said: 'By then you have reached a signpost,' Marple realised that their leg was being well and truly pulled so laconically one member interrupted:

'That's a pity because I can't read.'

You never, however, catch a Buxworth man lost for words and quick as a flash came the reply:

'That'll do for you then, 'cos there's nothing on it.'

Oh yes, they are characters all right these cricketers from the hills and as sharp as they make them. There's a Tommy Higginbottom who earned immortality by racing on to the pitch clad only in his shirt in his efforts to save High Lane from defeat.

He was captaining the team who were in the not unknown position of having only 10 men and the equally not unknown position of struggling.

Facing a huge score the tenth and last batsman had gone out and Tommy was changing when he suddenly remembered the scorer. A message was sent round for him to come and sort out some kit and be ready to bat but before the boy could even get to the pavilion the ninth wicket had fallen. Thinking that the game was over the stumps were being pulled and the players walking off when Tommy, shirt-tail streaming behind him, ran out yelling: 'Get back, get back, we're batting the scorer.'

I would like to be able to report that Tommy's enterprise saved the day. Alas no, but his wit and quick-thinking did save an awkward situation when he later turned to umpiring.

The batsman he had given out refused to go.

'I'm not out and I'm not going,' he said, and a nasty situation was building up as the batsman stood his ground. To which Tommy merely countered: 'And if the next batsman isn't here within two minutes he will be out, too.'

Umpiring can have its quixotic moments in these parts for these dedicated men are as much part of the atmosphere as the players. Take the day when a runner was given out.

If an infallible plan of operating with a runner has ever been devised—and I doubt it—then we haven't heard of it round here. In this game there was the inevitable mix-up with the air thick with conflicting calls. 'Yes', 'Howd on', 'Yes', 'No . . .', 'Of course', 'Wait', 'Come on', 'Go back', and, finally, 'Oh, blast'.

A clear case of run out and the batsman and his runner started trudging off.

'Not you, you stay there', said the umpire, pointing to the surprised batsman and, switching his finger to the runner, he added: 'It's him that's out.'

The eccentricities even spread to the local sports shops as was discovered by John Massey, an opening bat of Norbury who judges his success in length of time at the wicket, rather than runs made. 'A pair of batting gloves—left handed', he asked the shop assistant.

'Oh no, sir, you don't catch me like that'.

'Like what?'

'Left handed gloves indeed, oh dear me no! You can't catch me.'

Nor could Massey—even with demonstrations of left handed and right handed batting much to the amazement and amusement of other customers—persuade the assistant that there was such a thing.

I wouldn't, however, want my countless cricketing friends in this area to get the wrong idea and think that I am laughing at them. The truth is that I am laughing with them for this is my kind of cricket—and to prove it I suffered for it last summer. Stanton-in-the-Peak was my Waterloo. Now there's a ground for you, Stanton that is, not Waterloo. On a fine day from what seems to be a ledge near the summit of a hill you have a magnificent panorama of the Bakewell area; otherwise you can make a close study of cloud formations. There's none of your nonsense here about tea between innings. They do the job properly by having a fixed time. The reason, however, is more unusual for it is rumoured that it is to enable the ladies to get to church in time.

When I limped home that night my wife pronounced my injury as retribution for having cut short our annual holiday to play. On inspecting the swollen ankle she further triumphantly announced: 'I'll send all your kit to the cleaners tomorrow—you won't want it any more this season.'

The next day the doctor at the Manchester Royal Infirmary confided that I had a torn ligament, a chipped bone and the flattest feet he had ever seen. Fame at last. All the nurses were invited to inspect my feet like some rare specimens, and not until then was my right leg plastered up.

Back home on crutches my wife added: 'I needn't have bothered with the cleaners—you won't want your kit any more at all.'

I know better. I'll be there again this season at those delightful villages where men are cricketers and the women know their place in life—to make cricketing teas. This is the game they play with just as much enthusiasm as Jack Bond and his boys. And don't tell me that cricket is dead for within five miles radius of my home I could play on a different pitch on every Sunday of the season. Now there's an idea. . . .

# JOHN PLAYER SUNDAY LEAGUE TABLE 1970

*Points awarded*   WIN (4)   NO RESULT (1)

| | *Played* | *Won* | *Lost* | *No result* | *Points* | *Run rate per over* |
|---|---|---|---|---|---|---|
| LANCASHIRE (1) | 16 | 13 | 2 | 1 | 53 | — |
| KENT (4) | 16 | 12 | 4 | 0 | 48 | — |
| DERBYSHIRE (15) | 16 | 11 | 5 | 0 | 44 | — |
| ESSEX (3) | 16 | 8 | 5 | 3 | 35 | — |
| WARWICKSHIRE (9) | 16 | 8 | 6 | 2 | 34 | — |
| WORCESTERSHIRE (12) | 16 | 8 | 7 | 1 | 33 | — |
| LEICESTERSHIRE (11) | 16 | 7 | 7 | 2 | 30 | 4.56 |
| GLOUCESTERSHIRE (6) | 16 | 7 | 7 | 2 | 30 | 4.34 |
| SURREY (5) | 16 | 7 | 7 | 2 | 30 | 4.16 |
| NOTTINGHAMSHIRE (13) | 16 | 7 | 9 | 0 | 28 | — |
| MIDDLESEX (7) | 16 | 6 | 8 | 2 | 26 | — |
| HAMPSHIRE (2) | 16 | 6 | 10 | 0 | 24 | 4.60 |
| NORTHAMPTONSHIRE (14) | 16 | 6 | 10 | 0 | 24 | 4.17 |
| YORKSHIRE (8) | 16 | 5 | 9 | 2 | 22 | 4.20 |
| SOMERSET (16) | 16 | 5 | 9 | 2 | 22 | 4.09 |
| GLAMORGAN (10) | 16 | 5 | 9 | 2 | 22 | 3.85 |
| SUSSEX (17) | 16 | 3 | 10 | 3 | 15 | — |

*Figures in brackets indicate 1969 positions*

## FINAL CHAMPIONSHIP TABLE

| Points awarded | Played | Won 10. | Lost | Drawn | Bonus points Batting | Bonus points Bowling | Points | Up or down |
|---|---|---|---|---|---|---|---|---|
| 1 KENT (10) | 24 | 9 | 5 | 10 | 70 | 77 | 237 | — |
| 2 GLAMORGAN (1) | 24 | 9 | 6 | 9 | 48 | 82 | 220 | — |
| 3 LANCASHIRE (15) | 24 | 6 | 2 | 16 | 78 | 78 | 216 | +6 |
| 4 YORKSHIRE (13) | 24 | 8 | 5 | 11 | 49 | 86 | 215 | — |
| 5 SURREY (3) | 24 | 6 | 4 | 14 | 60 | 83 | 203 | —2 |
| 6 WORCESTERSHIRE (12) | 24 | 7 | 1 | 16 | 46 | 84 | 200 | —2 |
| 7 DERBYSHIRE (16) | 24 | 7 | 7 | 10 | 51 | 78 | 199 | —2 |
| 8 WARWICKSHIRE (4) | 24 | 7 | 6 | 11 | 53 | 71 | 199 | —4 |
| 9 SUSSEX (7) | 24 | 5 | 7 | 12 | 62 | 87 | 199 | —1 |
| 10 HAMPSHIRE (5) | 24 | 4 | 6 | 14 | 69 | 88 | 197 | — |
| 11 NOTTINGHAMSHIRE (8) | 24 | 4 | 8 | 12 | 71 | 73 | 184 | — |
| 12 ESSEX (6) | 24 | 4 | 6 | 14 | 64 | 76 | 180 | +1 |
| 13 SOMERSET (17) | 24 | 5 | 10 | 9 | 40 | 86 | 176 | —1 |
| 14 NORTHAMPTONSHIRE (9) | 24 | 4 | 6 | 14 | 60 | 74 | 174 | — |
| 15 LEICESTERSHIRE (14) | 24 | 5 | 6 | 13 | 46 | 77 | 173 | +1 |
| 16 MIDDLESEX (11) | 24 | 5 | 5 | 14 | 47 | 69 | 166 | — |
| 17 GLOUCESTERSHIRE (2) | 24 | 3 | 8 | 13 | 56 | 80 | 166 | +1 |

Warwickshire's record includes five points in drawn match when scores finished level and they were batting.

Figures in brackets indicate 1969 positions.

# JOHN PLAYER LEAGUE AVERAGES—BOWLING

(*Qualification:* 20 WICKETS: AVERAGE 16.50)

| Name | Overs | Maidens | Runs | Wickets | Average |
|------|-------|---------|------|---------|---------|
| K. Shuttleworth | 92.1 | 15 | 265 | 24 | 11.04 |
| K. D. Boyce | 95.3 | 15 | 347 | 28 | 12.39 |
| J. Simmons | 98.5 | 7 | 366 | 26 | 14.07 |
| D. P. Hughes | 83.4 | 7 | 348 | 24 | 14.50 |
| A. N. Connolly | 93.2 | 14 | 333 | 21 | 15.85 |
| G. D. McKenzie | 100.5 | 14 | 313 | 20 | 15.65 |
| V. A. Holder | 104 | 12 | 339 | 21 | 16.14 |
| D. J. Brown | 93.4 | 7 | 359 | 22 | 16.31 |
| B. S. Crump | 105 | 15 | 343 | 21 | 16.33 |

## JOHN PLAYER LEAGUE AVERAGES—BATTING

(*Qualification:* 8 COMPLETED INNINGS: AVERAGE 43.00)

| Name | Inns. | Not out | Runs | Highest Inns. | Average |
|---|---|---|---|---|---|
| B. A. Richards | 11 | 2 | 592 | 155* | 65.77 |
| C. H. Lloyd | 14 | 5 | 521 | 134* | 57.88 |
| H. Pilling | 15 | 3 | 625 | 85 | 52.08 |
| B. W. Luckhurst | 11 | 1 | 520 | 142 | 52.00 |
| M. J. Harris | 16 | 3 | 595 | 104* | 45.76 |
| B. A. Davis | 13 | 1 | 335 | 74 | 44.58 |
| W. E. Russell | 9 | 1 | 348 | 68 | 43.50 |
| M. J. K. Smith | 13 | 3 | 434 | 91* | 43.40 |
| M. H. Denness | 16 | 2 | 582 | 94* | 41.57 |

\* Signifies not out.

# SUNDAY LEAGUE AWARDS 1970

A TOTAL OF 434 SIXES WERE HIT DURING THE SEASON
Each was worth £2 6s. 1d.

LEADING SIX HITTERS:
17—S. E. Leary (KENT)
15—C. H. Lloyd (LANCASHIRE)
13—B. W. Luckhurst (KENT)
12—H. M. Ackerman (NORTHAMPTONSHIRE), P. T. Marner (LEICESTERSHIRE)
  and B. A. Richards (HAMPSHIRE)
9—K. D. Boyle (ESSEX), M. J. Harris (NOTTINGHAMSHIRE), J. Sullivan
  (LANCASHIRE) and J. D. Woodford (YORKSHIRE)
8—A. E. Cordle (GLAMORGAN), R. E. Marshall (HAMPSHIRE) and C. P.
  Wilkins (DERBYSHIRE)

FOUR OR MORE WICKETS IN AN INNINGS WAS COMPLETED 58 TIMES
Each being worth £17 4s. 11d.

BOWLERS WHO PERFORMED THE FEAT TWICE ARE:
D. Breakwell (NORTHAMPTONSHIRE), M. J. Bore (YORKSHIRE),
R. G. M. Carter (WORCESTERSHIRE), A. N. Connolly (MIDDLESEX),
D. J. Halfyard (NOTTINGHAMSHIRE), D. P. Hughes (LANCASHIRE),
P. Lever (LANCASHIRE), P. H. Parfitt (MIDDLESEX), D. R. Smith
(GLOUCESTERSHIRE) and D. L. Underwood (KENT).

THIRTY-EIGHT BOWLERS TOOK FOUR OR MORE WICKETS ONCE.

# LANCASHIRE AVERAGES IN FIRST CLASS MATCHES 1970
## BATTING

|  | No. Inns. | Times N.O. | H.S. | Total runs | Averages |
|---|---|---|---|---|---|
| C. H. Lloyd | 28 | 2 | 163 | 1203 | 46.26 |
| B. Wood | 44 | 7 | 144 | 1457 | 39.37 |
| H. Pilling | 41 | 7 | 120* | 1315 | 38.67 |
| F. Hayes | 22 | 3 | 99 | 719 | 37.84 |
| K. Snellgrove | 14 | 1 | 138 | 474 | 36.46 |
| J. D. Bond | 33 | 9 | 89 | 780 | 32.50 |
| D. Lloyd | 39 | 4 | 124 | 1039 | 29.68 |
| F. M. Engineer | 33 | 4 | 89 | 797 | 27.48 |
| J. Sullivan | 32 | 3 | 72 | 669 | 23.06 |
| P. Lever | 12 | 7 | 26* | 112 | 22.40 |
| J. Simmons | 28 | 8 | 112 | 423 | 21.15 |
| D. P. Hughes | 28 | 9 | 55 | 343 | 18.05 |
| K. Shuttleworth | 14 | 7 | 20 | 114 | 16.28 |
| K. Goodwin | 6 | 2 | 6 | 16 | 4.00 |
| P. Gooch | 3 | 1 | 0* | — | — |
| *Also batted* | | | | | |
| A. Kennedy | 2 | 1 | 25 | 26 | 26.00 |
| M. Staziker | 2 | 2 | 1* | 1 | — |

## BOWLING

|  | Overs | Maidens | Runs | Wickets | Average |
|---|---|---|---|---|---|
| B. Wood | 287 | 80 | 601 | 31 | 19.38 |
| J. Sullivan | 183 | 51 | 470 | 22 | 21.36 |
| K. Shuttleworth | 596 | 145 | 1599 | 74 | 21.60 |
| P. Lever | 647 | 163 | 1657 | 76 | 21.80 |
| D. P. Hughes | 803 | 248 | 2377 | 82 | 28.98 |
| C. H. Lloyd | 270 | 72 | 698 | 22 | 31.72 |
| J. Simmons | 559 | 153 | 1478 | 40 | 36.95 |
| P. Gooch | 83 | 18 | 252 | 6 | 42.00 |
| D. Lloyd | 93 | 27 | 316 | 7 | 45.14 |
| M. Staziker | 57 | 11 | 269 | 1 | 269.00 |
| *Also bowled* | | | | | |
| F. M. Engineer | 4 | 1 | 10 | 0 | — |
| F. Hayes | 7 | 3 | 10 | 0 | — |
| H. Pilling | 0 | 0 | 4 | 0 | — |

# LANCASHIRE AVERAGES IN FIRST CLASS MATCHES 1970
## CATCHES

| | |
|---|---|
| J. D. Bond | 24 |
| F. Hayes | 18 |
| D. Lloyd | 18 |
| J. Sullivan | 18 |
| D. Hughes | 16 |
| B. Wood | 15 |
| P. Lever | 12 |
| C. H. Lloyd | 10 |
| J. Simmons | 9 |
| H. Pilling | 8 |
| K. Shuttleworth | 5 |
| K. Snellgrove | 3 |
| P. Gooch | 3 |

## WICKET KEEPERS

| | *Caught* | *Stumped* |
|---|---|---|
| F. M. Engineer | 78 | 4 |
| K. Goodwin | 12 | 2 |

# LANCASHIRE AVERAGES IN GILLETTE CUP MATCHES 1970

PLAYED 4   WON 4

## BATTING

|  | No. Inns. | Not out | H.S. | Total runs | Averages |
|---|---|---|---|---|---|
| B. Wood | 4 | 1 | 63* | 153 | 51.00 |
| J. D. Bond | 3 | 2 | 35* | 40 | 40.00 |
| C. H. Lloyd | 4 | 0 | 53 | 157 | 39.25 |
| H. Pilling | 4 | 1 | 70* | 114 | 38.00 |
| D. Lloyd | 2 | 0 | 62 | 74 | 37.00 |
| J. Sullivan | 4 | 0 | 50 | 130 | 32.50 |
| F. M. Engineer | 4 | 1 | 35 | 91 | 30.33 |
| D. P. Hughes | 2 | 1 | 8 | 14 | 14.00 |
| F. Hayes | 2 | 0 | 0 | 0 | — |
| J. Simmons | 1 | 1 | 14 | 14 | — |
| P. Lever | 1 | 1 | 1* | 1 | — |
| K. Shuttleworth | — | — | — | — | — |
| P. Gooch | — | — | — | — | — |

## BOWLING

|  | Overs | Maidens | Runs | Wickets | Average |
|---|---|---|---|---|---|
| B. Wood | 12 | 0 | 35 | 3 | 11.33 |
| K. Shuttleworth | 35 | 5 | 82 | 5 | 16.40 |
| P. Lever | 47 | 5 | 142 | 8 | 17.75 |
| D. P. Hughes | 38 | 3 | 125 | 6 | 20.83 |
| C. H. Lloyd | 39 | 5 | 149 | 6 | 24.83 |
| J. Simmons | 39 | 2 | 129 | 4 | 32.25 |
| J. Sullivan | 7 | 0 | 42 | 1 | 42.00 |
| P. Gooch | 10 | 2 | 40 | 0 | — |

# LANCASHIRE AVERAGES IN JOHN PLAYER LEAGUE 1970
## BATTING

|  | No. Inns. | Not out | H.S. | Total runs | Averages |
|---|---|---|---|---|---|
| C. H. Lloyd | 14 | 5 | 134* | 521 | 57.88 |
| H. Pilling | 15 | 3 | 85 | 625 | 52.08 |
| J. Sullivan | 14 | 5 | 76* | 364 | 40.44 |
| F. Hayes | 4 | 1 | 53 | 111 | 37.00 |
| K. Snellgrove | 8 | 0 | 59 | 238 | 29.75 |
| D. Lloyd | 9 | 1 | 98 | 221 | 27.62 |
| F. M. Engineer | 15 | 0 | 57 | 340 | 22.66 |
| J. D. Bond | 10 | 4 | 33 | 110 | 18.33 |
| B. Wood | 8 | 3 | 28 | 79 | 15.80 |
| P. Lever | 4 | 3 | 3* | 10 | 10.00 |
| D. P. Hughes | 5 | 1 | 19* | 35 | 8.75 |
| J. Simmons | 6 | 1 | 22 | 38 | 7.60 |
| *Also batted* | | | | | |
| K. Shuttleworth | 2 | 1 | 17* | 33 | 33.00 |
| M. Staziker | 1 | 1 | 0 | 0 | 0.00 |
| K. Goodwin | 1 | — | — | — | — |

## BOWLING

|  | Overs | Maidens | Runs | Wickets | Averages |
|---|---|---|---|---|---|
| K. Shuttleworth | 92 | 15 | 265 | 24 | 11.04 |
| J. Simmons | 100 | 7 | 366 | 26 | 14.07 |
| B. Wood | 33 | 3 | 144 | 10 | 14.40 |
| D. P. Hughes | 83 | 7 | 348 | 24 | 14.50 |
| P. Lever | 103 | 11 | 364 | 21 | 17.33 |
| C. H. Lloyd | 62 | 2 | 266 | 10 | 26.60 |
| J. Sullivan | 21 | 3 | 112 | 2 | 56.00 |
| *Also bowled* | | | | | |
| H. Pilling | 1 | 0 | 3 | 2 | 1.50 |
| M. J. Staziker | 8 | 0 | 29 | 1 | 29.00 |